IMAGES
of America

TEXON

LEGACY OF AN OIL TOWN

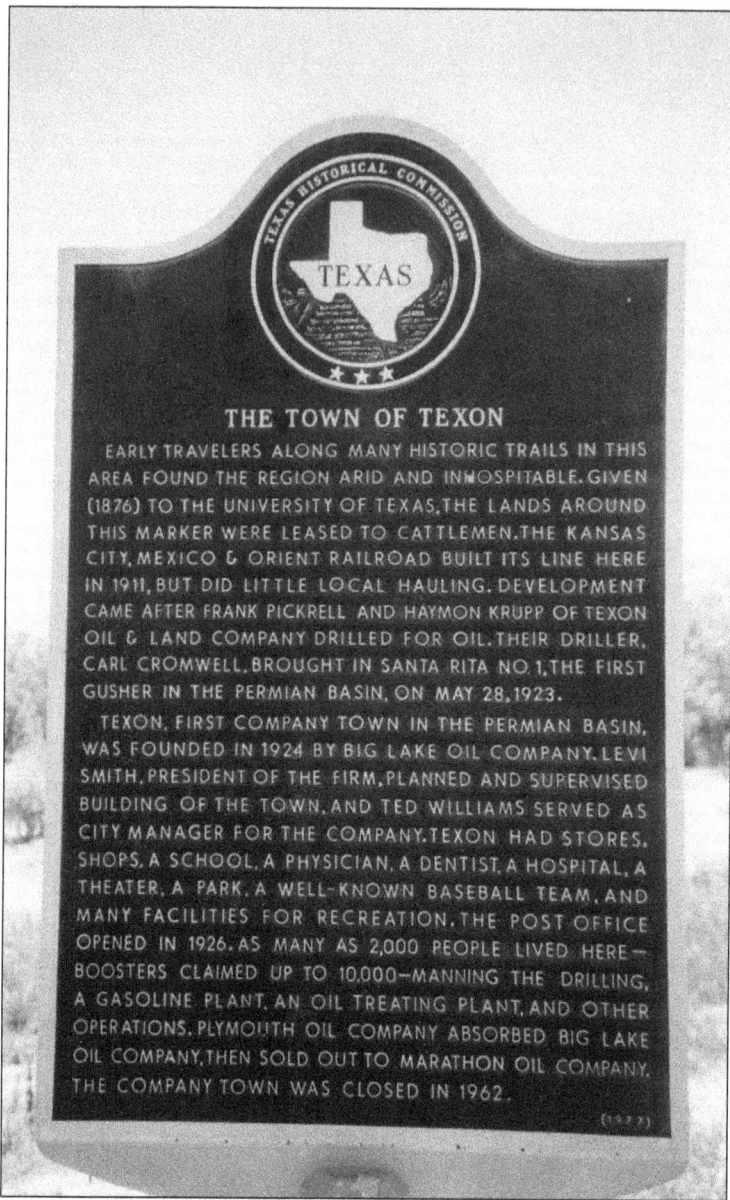

THE TOWN OF TEXON

EARLY TRAVELERS ALONG MANY HISTORIC TRAILS IN THIS AREA FOUND THE REGION ARID AND INHOSPITABLE. GIVEN (1876) TO THE UNIVERSITY OF TEXAS, THE LANDS AROUND THIS MARKER WERE LEASED TO CATTLEMEN. THE KANSAS CITY, MEXICO & ORIENT RAILROAD BUILT ITS LINE HERE IN 1911, BUT DID LITTLE LOCAL HAULING. DEVELOPMENT CAME AFTER FRANK PICKRELL AND HAYMON KRUPP OF TEXON OIL & LAND COMPANY DRILLED FOR OIL. THEIR DRILLER, CARL CROMWELL, BROUGHT IN SANTA RITA NO 1, THE FIRST GUSHER IN THE PERMIAN BASIN, ON MAY 28, 1923.

TEXON, FIRST COMPANY TOWN IN THE PERMIAN BASIN, WAS FOUNDED IN 1924 BY BIG LAKE OIL COMPANY. LEVI SMITH, PRESIDENT OF THE FIRM, PLANNED AND SUPERVISED BUILDING OF THE TOWN, AND TED WILLIAMS SERVED AS CITY MANAGER FOR THE COMPANY. TEXON HAD STORES, SHOPS, A SCHOOL, A PHYSICIAN, A DENTIST, A HOSPITAL, A THEATER, A PARK, A WELL-KNOWN BASEBALL TEAM, AND MANY FACILITIES FOR RECREATION. THE POST OFFICE OPENED IN 1926. AS MANY AS 2,000 PEOPLE LIVED HERE—BOOSTERS CLAIMED UP TO 10,000—MANNING THE DRILLING, A GASOLINE PLANT, AN OIL TREATING PLANT, AND OTHER OPERATIONS. PLYMOUTH OIL COMPANY ABSORBED BIG LAKE OIL COMPANY, THEN SOLD OUT TO MARATHON OIL COMPANY. THE COMPANY TOWN WAS CLOSED IN 1962.

(1977)

This Texas Historical Commission historical marker was approved in 1977 and installed the same year on the south side of State Highway 67 at the turnoff to the Texon townsite. Doris Way and Velma Marshall, former Texon residents, prepared and submitted the application for the marker. (Photograph by James A. Wilson.)

ON THE COVER: The Texon Theatre, always called the "picture show," opened in early 1927, seated 400, and offered its first "talkie," *The Love Doctor* starring Richard Dix, in 1929. Its family-oriented programming not only included first-run films but also baby shows, money and dish giveaways, beauty contests, and performances by area musical groups. Texon boys and girls sold popcorn, operated the projectors, and cleaned for free passes. The theater meant much more than movies for 10¢ and 25¢; it was a mainstay of community life. The 1950 fire that destroyed it (after showing *The Rustlers*) claimed what resident June Barbee Bone called "the most appreciated place in town." (Ann Way Schneemann).

IMAGES
of America

TEXON
LEGACY OF AN OIL TOWN

Jane Spraggins Wilson
and James A. Wilson

ARCADIA
PUBLISHING

Published by Arcadia Publishing
Charleston, South Carolina

Library of Congress Control Number: 2011920844

For all general information, please contact Arcadia Publishing:
Telephone 843-853-2070
Fax 843-853-0044
E-mail sales@arcadiapublishing.com
For customer service and orders:
Toll-Free 1-888-313-2665

Visit us on the Internet at www.arcadiapublishing.com

*In loving memory of my parents, Bill and Bernice Spraggins,
and my brother Marion. With love and devotion to my brothers,
R.W. and Rex, and my sister, Ann. With love and gratitude to
Tug, my partner in life and in the writing of this book, without
whom it would not have happened. With love and devotion to our
children, Wesley, Linda and Jeff, and Kevin and Cindy; and to
our grandchildren, Courtney, Dale, Paul, Ryan, and Leslie.*

CONTENTS

ACKNOWLEDGMENTS

So many Texon friends shared their memories, pictures, and stories with me that there is not space to name them all. Not to mention them does not lessen the importance of their contributions. I would be remiss if I didn't recognize four men who, over the long period of my researching, continued to offer information and encouragement. They are H.L. "Bob" Adams, Hal Burton, W.L. "Whitey" Grissett, and Randolph S. "Randy" King. In Midland, Whitey and Fay Grissett opened their home for several weekend stays and delicious meals, and Fay provided her perspective on Texon. Randy's home in Sinton was the setting for my interview with Mary Griffith and former Texon men Plymouth transferred to Sinton. In addition, during the actual writing of the book, Gene Cook was invaluable because of his long tenure with the Big Lake, Plymouth, and Marathon companies and his exceptional memory of the field, town, and events. He was always fun to consult when snags occurred. Thanks, Gene. Through the years, Donald Meroney and lifelong friend Maxine Adams Hyden have also been pleasant sources of information. Thanks to both. To Lauren Hummer, of Arcadia Publishing, goes a special thank you for her patience, encouragement, and kindness. Leslie Meyer, director of archives and collections at the Petroleum Museum in Midland, was immensely helpful with images of Texon from the museum's treasures. With her friendly manner and professionalism, she was a joy to work with. Suzanne Campbell, director of the West Texas Collection, Angelo State University, has lent professionalism and encouragement to my research. To my great surprise and delight, John Carroll of Keaton Kolor, San Angelo, had his own connection to Texon. His artistic work with photographs has certainly added to the beauty of this book. All photographs by W.L. "Bill" Thompson are courtesy of Paul C. "Buzz" Crews. Thanks to Buzz for allowing unfettered use of his uncle's photographs. If a picture of your favorite person or event is not included, I share your disappointment because I experienced the same. In the end, the available images were in my collection or borrowed from others.

From the moment I said I wanted to write a history of Texon, my husband, Tug, has been an active supporter and participant. He has added the necessary professionalism to the project and, after 40 years of reunions and Texon talk, should be deemed a Texonite. It has been fun and rewarding. Thanks, Tug. As an adult, it was extremely satisfying getting to know Texon people I had known only as a child. Through the whole process, I relived the Texon experience, which solidified my long-held opinion that I was fortunate to have grown up among such good people in a special place.

—Jane Spraggins Wilson

Abbreviations for frequently cited photograph credits are: Lilla Beyer Carter (LBC), John David Grissett collection (JDG), Bill Thompson (BT), and the Jane Spraggins Wilson collection (JSW).

INTRODUCTION

For nearly 40 years, Texon was a company oil town with its existence dependent upon a nonrenewable resource. The Texon Oil and Land Company successfully drilled the Santa Rita No. 1 well in May 1923 in Reagan County. The discovery set off a boom in West Texas and began the flow of royalty wealth from the Permian Basin to the University of Texas. Michael Benedum and Joseph C. Trees (B-T), both of Pittsburgh, bought more than 10,000 acres of the Texon Company's leases, brought in wells that revealed a profitable pool of oil, and formed the Plymouth Oil Company, whose subsidiary, the Big Lake Oil Company (BLOC), developed the Big Lake Field. Levi Smith, BLOC president and general manager, was determined to provide a stable environment for employees and their families. In 1924–1925, his vision resulted in the building of Texon.

The BLOC—the "company"—represented opportunity. Of the approximately 1,150 who lived in Texon in 1930, about 60 percent came from Texas. Here, as in the entire country, agriculture was depressed in the 1920s, and the oil patch offered relief from 5¢ and 6¢ cotton. The majority of other workers were Oklahomans and West Virginians, many of them seasoned oil field workers who proved invaluable. However, many were inexperienced. One early gang pusher (foreman) recalled that "farm boys" were "used to manual labor" and made better hands than dismounted "cowpokes." Continuous drilling of new wells boosted output to more than nine million barrels in 1932, the year of Levi Smith's death. But Smith's successor, Charles E. Beyer, faced a steady decline, and production in 1941 barely exceeded two million. During the mid-1930s, Plymouth Oil developed new properties and transferred to them workers from Texon, whose estimated population fell to 800 in 1940 and 470 in 1945. After World War II, the Big Lake Field was essentially a maintenance operation. From 1945 through 1961, the number of wells fell from 192 to 145, and production decreased by more than half. In the late 1940s, Plymouth opened fields in Upton and Tom Green Counties, which drew more residents from Texon; took control of BLOC in 1956; and watched its bottom line deteriorate. In 1962, Plymouth sold out to Marathon Oil, ending company support for Texon.

Levi Smith created Texon, which journalists were soon calling a "model" oil town. His influence, often applied by his detail-minded assistant Ted Williams, seemed to touch every part of community life. Given Texon's isolation, it enjoyed amenities—including the company-built church, hospital, elementary school, theater, golf course, and baseball field for the beloved Oilers—that West Texans envied. Smith's appealing personality and Labor Day celebrations advertised Texon and promoted goodwill throughout the area. His death in 1932 began the town's second phase, which extended through the 1930s to the end of World War II. Although the Depression gripped the state and country, Texon continued to thrive. Social organizations appealed to every taste. The Texon Union Church, the clubhouse, and the Joe C. Trees swimming pool vibrated with activity. The Texon School, with its harmonica and rhythm bands and dedicated teachers, was a source of pride, and Scout groups for boys and girls received company support and guidance from adults. During the war, Texon typified patriotism. Its men and women in uniform, bond and scrap-iron drives, Home Guard unit, countless volunteer hours, and Charles Beyer's generosity toward service personnel all placed Texon's people in the ranks of the "Greatest Generation."

Unsuccessful wartime drilling indicated that the period of 1946 to 1962 would be Texon's last. Beyer retired in 1950, the same year the hospital closed and the theater burned. Houses were moved to new camps, the gas plant closed in 1952, and retirements and transfers made a small town smaller. But those who stayed stood tall. They maintained the church, supported Scout groups and junior baseball, and extended a helping hand to flood victims. They also enjoyed the arrival of dial telephones (1947) and television, golf at the Colina Alta course, and trap shooting. To the end, they were community-minded.

Soon after Plymouth's sale, Marathon employees who chose to stay received leases from University of Texas Lands and lived on the townsite for several years. Those remaining couples were among the organizers of the Texon reunions, which began in 1964 and continue to the present.

One

THE EARLY YEARS

Texon's beginnings—1924 to 1932—were the direct result of the oil boom generated by Santa Rita No. 1 and the constructive imagination of Levi Smith. As president and general manager of the Big Lake Oil Company, Smith developed the Big Lake Field at a furious clip, which made a growing work force necessary. His years of experience in rowdy oil camps inspired him to plan and create a company town where employees and their families could live safely and comfortably.

And so, in the mid-1920s, Texon came to life. Its location, on the calcified, mesquite-strewn Edwards Plateau of Reagan County in West Texas, was 14 miles west of Big Lake, a ranching town of some 100 souls that became the county seat in 1925 because of its oil-generated growth. The nearest commercial hub was San Angelo, 84 miles to the east, whose post–Santa Rita population swelled. Because of Texon's isolation, Smith ensured that his employees' families had access to medical, educational, and recreational facilities seldom found in a rural setting. "Texon, almost from its establishment, has enjoyed most of the conveniences of a larger town," complimented the *San Angelo Daily Standard* on May 10, 1925. Also remarkable were the community's peaceful atmosphere and traditional activities that contrasted sharply with the goings-on in Best, the nearby oil field supply center.

Smith's death in 1932 left residents in shock. They had lost the man who for many was a father figure. That feeling was natural, since virtually every facet of life in Texon reflected his attention to detail and concern for those who depended upon him. For instance, as the Great Depression tightened its grip on Texas, Smith, with the agreement of his men, implemented a policy of reducing hours, and thus wages, to create more work and avoid layoffs. In spite of the worsening economy, Smith's model company town—the product of his leadership—rested on a solid foundation.

On May 28, 1923, in Reagan County, driller Carl Cromwell brought in Santa Rita No. 1, the discovery well on the University of Texas's lands in the Permian Basin. The Texon Oil and Land Company had acquired the leases of Rupert Ricker, accepted the site selection of geologist Hugh Tucker, and hired Cromwell to begin drilling in January 1921. The well, which Catholic investors named for the Saint of the Impossible, gushed out of control for more than a month before it was "shut in." This spectacle heralded tremendous wealth for the University of Texas and its ramshackle Austin campus. (Left, JSW; below, map by Paul E. Daugherty.)

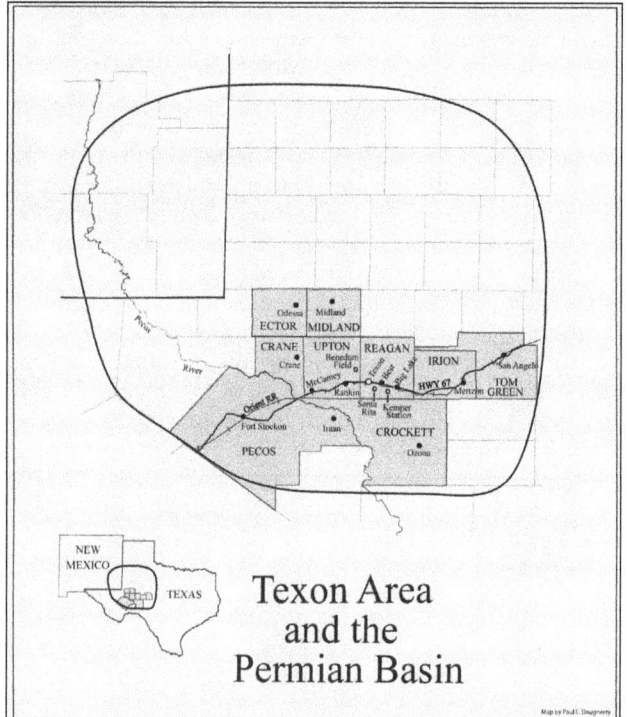

Texon Area
and the
Permian Basin

Levi Smith, born in Pennsylvania (1869) and raised in West Virginia, met Mike Benedum while both were Standard Oil employees. Like Benedum (right), Smith was largely self-educated and a devout Protestant. In the late 1890s, Smith joined B-T, on whose behalf he managed operations in six states; directed wildcatting in Romania's Ploesti Field; established strong ties with the flamboyant Queen Marie; and headed the Penn-Mex Fuel Company in revolutionary Mexico, where he worked with Charles E. Beyer and M.R. "Ted" Williams, who were later trusted associates. An avid baseball fan and golfer, he wrote poetry, loved classical music and great books, and flavored his correspondence with literary quotations. Seemingly unsuited for West Texas, his humanity, square dealing, and remarkable achievements proved otherwise. (Hal Burton.)

The Santa Rita aroused interest. In October 1923, the well's owner, the financially depleted Texon Company, sold 16 sections of its leases from the University of Texas to Michael L. Benedum and Joseph C. Trees (B-T), renowned Pittsburgh wildcatters, for cash and a quarter interest in the Big Lake Oil Company (BLOC). BLOC, a subsidiary of Texas-centered holding company Plymouth Oil, was formed to develop the Texon Company's leases. Its president, Levi Smith, who was a longtime B-T associate, had strongly encouraged the venture. He served with vice presidents Frank T. Pickrell and John M. Holliday, treasurer J.G. Farquhar, and secretary E.C. Stearns. By December, BLOC's temporary office was in San Angelo until permanent headquarters (above) were completed in Texon. (Hal Burton.)

Pulling tools from #18

Smith took over as BLOC's general manager, drew proven coworkers from the B-T organization, and undertook aggressive drilling. Well No. 4 began flowing in April 1924 and indicated a large oil pool. Nos. 9 and 11 justified the gamble on Reagan County and its development in June and July. By mid-July, the Big Lake Field was producing 3,500 barrels a day, success that attracted major competitors like Standard, Humble, and Shell. No. 18 (left)—which was proclaimed West Texas's greatest well—flowed 8,753 barrels one day in April 1925 and reflected the field's mounting annual output, which went from 1.4 million barrels in 1924 to 10.9 in 1926, then to 6.7 in 1928 when BLOC controlled 145 producing wells. The Big Lake Field, America's first totally electrified field, also included a gasoline plant and witnessed the change from cable tool to rotary drilling. (JSW.)

While Smith developed the Big Lake Field, he built Texon from scratch. His years in unruly oil boomtowns convinced him that family-oriented stability promoted a loyal, productive work force. By spring 1924, drillers like B.L. Agnew and David "Dad" Workman provided living quarters for their crews, and a boardinghouse, filling station, and grocery store were operating. But as the field flourished, its payroll grew, and Smith's envisioned town took shape with sewer and water systems; electricity; sidewalks; graded, oiled, and named streets like Cactus, San Jacinto, and Texas; and employee housing. Housing evolved from tents to temporary houses to separate family residences. Smith, a widower, pictured with daughter Imogene Ransom and granddaughter Jane, lived at 298 Greasewood. By the end of 1926, Texon's population was 739. (LBC Collection, Petroleum Museum.)

Trucker W.H. "Jack" Ferguson noticed the spewing Santa Rita and, in June 1923, launched the first commercial enterprise in what would become Texon, which consisted of a tent where he sold sandwiches and cold drinks. He later expanded and added groceries, gasoline, and sundries. In 1925, BLOC erected a grocery store building that soon included dry goods on Texas Street, the location of Texon's businesses. Ferguson rented it until Rudolph Theis took over in 1927. Ferguson also operated a filling station and garage. Pictured above is Steve Baldwin, a Ferguson employee. (Maurine Sumrall Gravell.)

By April 1924, Mrs. Walter Mann's boardinghouse had 85 lodgers. As the Big Lake Field's only eating place, it offered good meals for 50¢. W.F. "Dad" and "Mom" Wright soon became owners and began operating the company-built Texon Café in 1925. As family housing became available, the boardinghouse closed, although BLOC provided two dormitories for single men. Both the boardinghouse and the café food won consistent praise. (Clyde Miller.)

In 1926, Willie McGonagle became postmaster of Texon's first post office, located in the rear of the drugstore. He served until 1929, when J. Edgar "Las Vegas Kim" Kimsey was appointed. Mail, the principal link with the outside when telephones and radios were not common, arrived twice daily on the Orient Railroad, and residents gathered while it was "put up." Area ranchers like W.H. Dixon and O.W. Parker also had boxes. Pictured is Eunice Jones. (R.W. Spraggins.)

Texon Drug, commonly called the "drugstore," was owned by Willie H. and Alma McGonagle and opened in 1925. In 1926, Alma, then the sole owner, hired the first pharmacist, H.K. Jones. The soda fountain became very popular, as did the punch board game that awarded prizes. The drugstore also stocked assorted gift items. Pictured is Ada Lee Gregg. (R.W. Spraggins.)

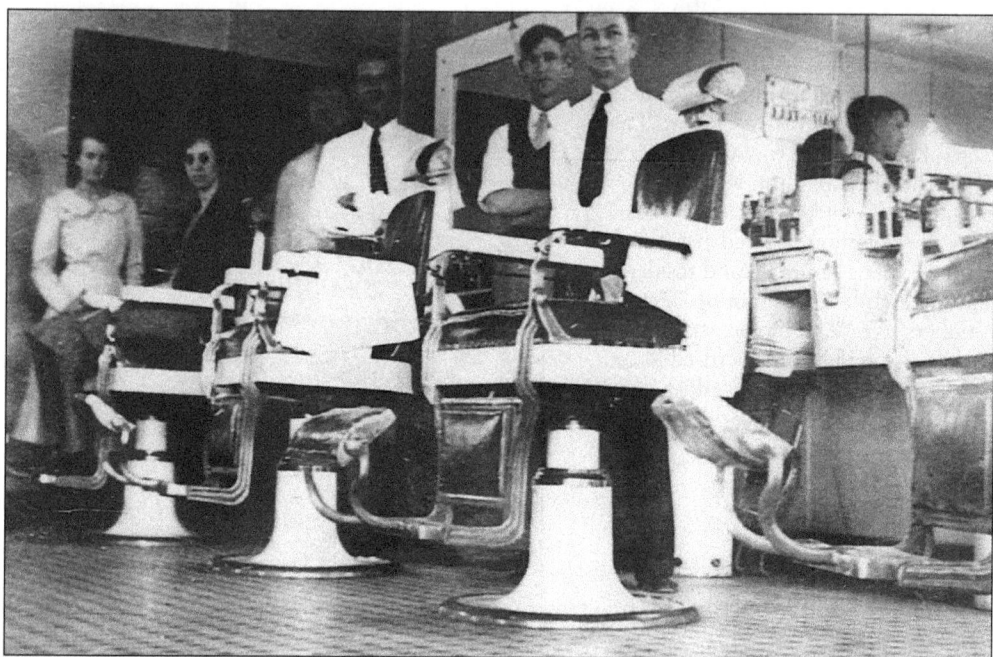

In the spring of 1926, barber Gabe Slaughter opened the Texon Barbershop. Oscar Lee (second from right) and Robert Lee Scott also cut hair, and Ike Chafin and Vonnie Brown were temporary employees. In the late 1920s, Ted Williams's Lone Star Industries, which briefly controlled Texon's businesses, bought the barber and tailor shops. (Ann Way Schneemann.)

The barbershop building also housed the first tailor shop, owned by Harold Tees. In 1931, Travis W. Cunningham (not the person pictured) offered cleaning, pressing, alterations, and delivery. In 1932, Mr. and Mrs. Aris Thorp assumed ownership of both shops and an owner's apartment. LaVerne Tatum's small beauty shop was added in 1930. (Ann Way Schneemann.)

The Santa Rita boom generated sufficient freight, passenger, and tank car traffic to save the ailing Kansas City, Mexico, and Orient Railway. In July 1924, the railway opened its Texon station in a boxcar with a telegraph. The boxcar also provided living quarters for agent J.J. Isbell and several of the earliest BLOC workers. A year later, passenger and mail service by motorcar (a gasoline-powered railcar) began. The Santa Fe Railway bought the now-profitable Orient Railway in 1929 and built a new station in 1930. The Santa Fe's motor train—affectionately called the "Doodlebug"—passed through Texon going from and to San Angelo twice daily. Fred R. Garver was the first Santa Fe agent. (Above, Clyde Miller; below, Arthur C. Flores.)

The company's icehouse, built in August 1924, stored ice hauled 33 miles from McCamey and later 84 miles from San Angelo. The big blocks were sawed into smaller blocks and delivered to the café, drug and grocery stores, hospital, and, during baseball season, to the grandstand's concession booth. For home delivery, square, colored cards numbered 25, 50, 75, and 100 pounds were positioned to show the number of the desired size. Employees were allowed to cool melons and meat in the icehouse. Below, the 1937 Chevrolet pickup's sideboard reads, "Those who know prefer ICE." The vehicle belonged to Perry Oaks, who operated the icehouse in the late 1930s and charged 20¢ for a 25-pound block. J.W. Eanes succeeded Oaks and subsequently sold out to Banner Creameries, which moved the building to Big Lake. (Above, Burke Isbell; below, Bob Talley.)

The Texon Volunteer Fire Department, manned by off-duty BLOC employees, was organized to battle blazes in the town and field. The first station—which ironically burned in 1925—housed two man-powered, two-wheeled carts, each with a fire extinguisher. Mounted on one cart was a reel of fire hose, and both carts carried hand extinguishers, shovels, and axes. Alongside the original station, which was located behind the café and boardinghouse, was a tall pole topped with a school bell that was rung when a fire was discovered. The second station, near the Texon Theatre, relied upon a 1932 Ford Model BB pumper-tank truck with tandem rear wheels, pictured after Marathon Oil acquired Plymouth in 1962. Its driver was the first man to reach the station. There was a central siren and several alarms placed around town. (Petroleum Museum.)

In October 1925, BLOC constructed a 60-by-100-foot vehicle storage garage north of the Orient track. Called the "Big Barn," it was a multiple-use facility and the venue for a summertime traveling roller rink, barbecues for dignitaries, boxing matches, various gymnasium sports, and, for several years, the company Christmas celebration. A strong wind collapsed it in 1954. (LBC.)

As Texon's first Christmas approached, Levi Smith sent employee W.M. "Mike" Griffith to Big Lake in the company's Star Touring Car to buy presents for the town's seven children. Another employee, costumed but naturally bearded, was the first Santa Claus. This 1924 gift giving began a tradition, which, in its early years, Smith personally funded. This cedar box is a gift from the late 1930s. (Photograph by Mary Stone; courtesy Linda Kaufmann.)

In 1924–1925, Texon children attended school in nearby Best. In October 1925, BLOC's two-room, two-teacher Texon Elementary School opened with 20 students and included kindergarten through the seventh grade. Ted Williams was the director. Mrs. G.L. Thompson taught first through third grade, and Mrs. Matthews, then Mrs. C.E. Terrell, taught fourth through seventh grade. Mrs. Pat Hitt and Mrs. Bruce Hitt were kindergarten teachers. In 1926–1927, another building and two teachers were added, and the company school joined the newly created Reagan County Independent School District (ISD). By 1932, three buildings were combined into one, pictured below. High school students were bused to Big Lake. Beginning in 1935, Santa Rita students attended school in Texon. (Above, LBC Collection, Petroleum Museum; below, photograph by BT.)

On October 6, 1925, twenty-four adults and children, meeting in the newly completed school (pictured on the previous page), organized the Texon Sunday School. W.H. "Bill" Agnew was superintendent, assisted by H.H. Talley. Viola Talley, Phema Agnew, and George Stahlman were junior, intermediate, and adult class teachers, respectively. Over the following year, attendance averaged a remarkable 200 students and underscored the need for a church building, which BLOC provided. It was dedicated on September 26, 1926, as the interdenominational Texon Union Church (pictured). Members formed a choir, a women's club, and Bible study groups; arranged for pulpit speakers and revivals; and welcomed their first minister, the Reverend W.E. Sampson, in 1928. A fundraising campaign financed a Sunday school classroom, completed in 1930. That same year, Sampson left, and the Reverend A.E. Arnfield replaced him in 1931. (Maxine Adams Hyden.)

Completed in the summer of 1925, the company-built Texon Hospital was Reagan County's first. The medical doctor was P.H. Chilton, and the nurse superintendent was Molly Gray. Equipped with a modern operating room, an X-ray machine, and large radium lights, the hospital (above) served a broad West Texas area. In 1926, Dr. C.W. "Choc" McCollum, Texon's one and only dentist, arrived. He practiced general dentistry from his office in the hospital, doubled as the surgical anesthesiologist, and became a beloved, vital member of the community. O.R. Goodall succeeded Chilton in 1928, and C.W. Ory took over in 1929. BLOC provided houses for doctors (below) and nurses. The earliest nurses were Enola Johnson, Ione Williams, Lucille Williams, Holly Petty, Alma Fell, and Genevieve Scott. (Above, Velma Harvey; below, Dr. Glen Pearson.)

Levi Smith, like 1920s America, embraced baseball, and the loyal Pittsburgh Pirates fan decreed that the BLOC would field a semiprofessional club. In 1925, the first team (above), called the Big Lake Oilers, soon became the Texon Oilers. Most players were permanent employees. Some were college athletes, and a few had professional experience, like James P. "Snipe" Conley, a former Texas League spitball pitcher, who was named player-manager in 1930. (Hal Burton.)

In 1926, Smith authorized construction of a covered, 500-seat grandstand with a scoreboard, concession stand, and sound system. In late May, it was filled to capacity when visiting Plymouth and BLOC officials were treated to an Oilers doubleheader and barbecue. Acclaimed by a San Angelo journalist as "one of the best" in West Texas, the grandstand exemplified the quality of Texon's recreational facilities. (Photograph by BT.)

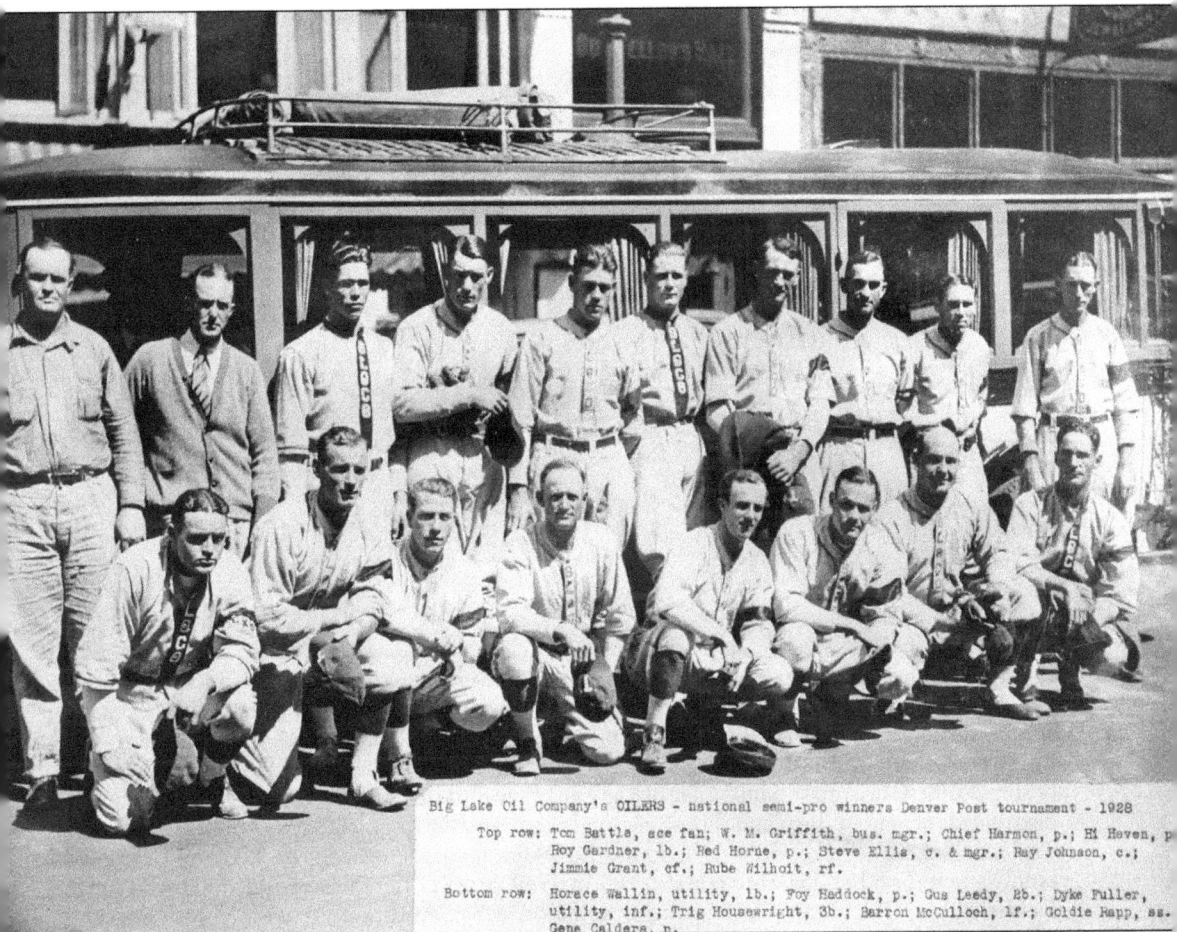

Big Lake Oil Company's OILERS - national semi-pro winners Denver Post tournament - 1928
Top row: Tom Battle, ace fan; W. M. Griffith, bus. mgr.; Chief Harmon, p.; Hi Heven, p
Roy Gardner, 1b.; Red Horne, p.; Steve Ellis, c. & mgr.; Ray Johnson, c.;
Jimmie Grant, cf.; Rube Wilhoit, rf.
Bottom row: Horace Wallin, utility, 1b.; Foy Haddock, p.; Gus Leedy, 2b.; Dyke Fuller,
utility, inf.; Trig Housewright, 3b.; Barron McCulloch, lf.; Goldie Rapp, ss.
Gene Caldera, p.

By 1928, the Oilers had compiled a winning record against West Texas competition. In August, they gained national stature by defeating the heavily favored Cheyenne Indians in the deciding game to win the *Denver Post*'s semiprofessional tournament that drew entries from 16 states. The Oilers placed four men on the all-tournament team and brought home a $4,000 cash prize and a trophy that was displayed in the Texon Drugstore. In the early 1930s, they continued to win and, along with Del Rio, dominated the West Texas League. They also took on the Texas League's Fort Worth Cats, another of Levi Smith's favorite ball clubs. Most importantly, the Oilers—who answered to "Flop," "Hi," "Putsy," and "Watermelon"—worked in the field and office, and they and their families were part of the Texon community. (JSW.)

In June 1929, Levi Smith purchased a six-seat Stinson Detroiter airplane with a 300-horsepower Wright J-6 engine. James J. Mattern, later a record-setting aviator, was Smith's first pilot, succeeded by son-in-law Ira E. "Shorty" Ransom, a World War I flier. Used for business and personal travel, the Detroiter also transported injured David Miller, son of BLOC engineer J.D. Miller, to a Dallas hospital. One Christmas, Santa Claus (Ransom) flew children's presents from Fort Worth and distributed them from the plane. Those pictured above are BLOC officials James S. Posgate, closest to plane, and E.C. "Spike" Stearns in boots; the others are unidentified. The 3,000-by-2,200-foot landing strip and hangar were constructed in 1929. Smith offered the commandant at Kelly Field, the Army Air Corps pilot training installation in San Antonio, use of the Texon "airport." (Both, Hal Burton.)

America's golf rage of the 1920s swept through Texon. In the summer of 1925, the original course was replaced with the Colina Alta (High Hill) Golf Club, named by Arthur C. Flores, the personal secretary to golfer Levi Smith. With a nine-hole, par-36 layout, its "greens" were pay-level (oily) sand before cottonseed hulls were laid in the spring of 1931. That year, the club hosted 52 entrants in its first invitational tournament, which included Calcutta betting and an awards banquet. Its eight-man team, anchored by phenom Jack Satterwhite and brothers Bob and Pat Kelly, won the Sand Belt Golf Association championship in a playoff with Colorado City on San Angelo Country Club's grass greens. Pictured are BLOC office employee Homer "Booger" Young teeing off and Arthur Flores just outside the golf shop. (Above, Hal Burton; right, John de la Garza.)

On October 14, 1930, touring golf professional Joe Kirkwood, a famed trick-shot artist whose son was later cast as Joe Palooka in film and television, played an exhibition on the Colina Alta course. About 250 tickets were sold for $1 each, and spectators from several towns braved a "blue norther." Winner of the Houston and Texas Opens, Kirkwood (putting above) did not disappoint. In a foursome with locals Fred Eberhardt and M.W. "Pee Wee" Whiteside and Al Badger, the San Angelo city champion, Kirkwood mastered the sand greens and blustery conditions for a course record 33. Golfer and stamp collector Jesse Thompson, who was also a BLOC office employee, sent the autographed envelope below to himself. (Above, photograph by BT; below, Jesse Thompson.)

In 1925, BLOC employees, including civil engineer Randolph "Randy" King and Arthur Flores, asked if tennis courts could be provided. Levi Smith agreed, and two enclosed courts were built and surfaced in pay-level sand that required frequent rolling and lining. Men, women, and children took up tennis, which became one of Texon's most popular sports. (Randy King.)

The Texon Tennis Association emerged. Its men's league teams included the Athletics, Cardinals, Pirates, and Senators. In early 1931, competition for the league title between the Cardinals and Pirates became so intense that spectators were alerted, humorously, to the possible danger of "hurtling rackets." Pictured are, from left to right, Harrie Smith, unidentified, Dick Callan, and captain of the Pirates Randy King. (Randy King.)

TEXON POLO CLUB   1930-31
Left to right
John Colbaugh   Ike Chaffin
Slats Baker   Shorty Arledge
Bill Lane   Called   Joe Carr
Cecil Brown (Mexican)   J. Edgar Kimsey
Mike Griffith

By 1928, Texon supported a polo team. In August 1930, it was judged "one of the fastest" in West Texas. Competition came from Midland, San Angelo, and San Antonio and from smaller towns like Fort Stockton, Menard, and Sterling City. Some matches were played on the oiled Texon airstrip. BLOC employees who were on the team furnished their own horses, feed, and transportation, and they were allowed time off for travel. An admission charge at both home and away matches helped defray expenses, and Texon organizations like the Boy Scouts sometimes received a percentage of the gate receipts. The polo club also sponsored popular dances. It remained active until 1934. In addition to those pictured, players included Irion County rancher Sonny Noelke and Captain Bloom, the team leader in 1932. (Ann Way Schneemann.)

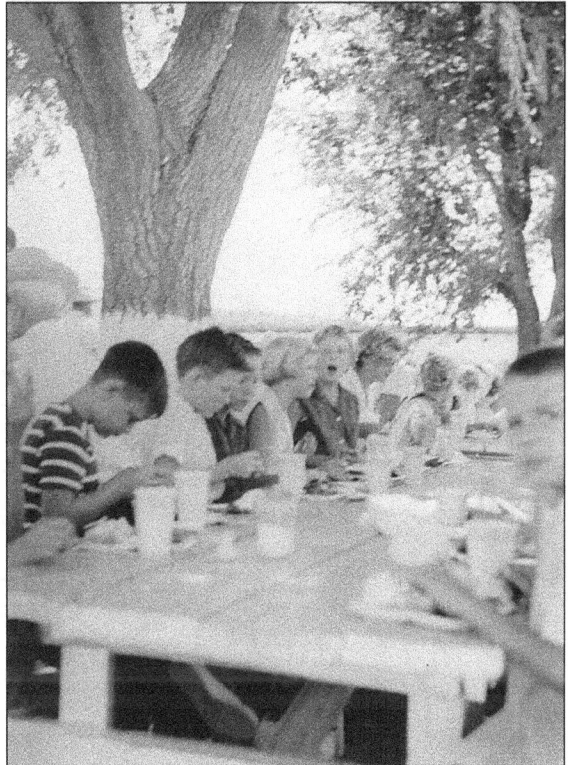

In 1929, in a grassy, shaded cove in the hills south of town, BLOC constructed a fenced picnic grounds with a large barbecue pit, tables, benches, and electric lights. Upon completion, the first annual Labor Day celebration—Levi Smith's king-sized goodwill gesture—was held, and everyone in the area was invited. Barbecued beef with all the trimmings was served to hundreds, and assistant general manager James S. Posgate distributed excess food to the county's needy. The weekend's activities included a rodeo, trap shooting, a special movie, a dance, and an Oilers game. It was an employee holiday, so only the most essential work went on. Another Texon tradition had begun, one that area neighbors and business people appreciated. (Both, Fay Grissett.)

Late in 1925, the company-built Texon Clubhouse (lower left) opened and quickly became the town's social center. Its two large, attractively furnished rooms, which were usually used for reading and recreation, could become—because of its polished maple floor—one big ballroom. There were two stone fireplaces and a slightly raised stage with a piano. The building hosted teas, bridge and Bible class parties, receptions, and organizational meetings like the 1925 gathering of the West Texas Petroleum Convention, chaired by Levi Smith. Dances were popular and frequent. Victrola dances charged minimally for admission, and there was a 5¢ fee for requested numbers; proceeds purchased new records. On special occasions like St. Patrick's Day and Christmas, couples enjoyed live music by such groups as the touring Nighthawk Serenaders from Shreveport and San Angelo's Keating Orchestra. (Mr. and Mrs. Roy Gardner Collection, Petroleum Museum.)

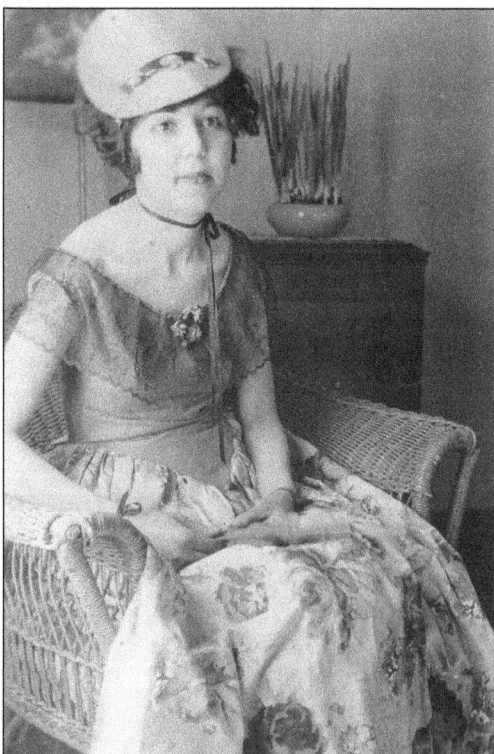

Early social activities varied. In November 1925, Arthur and Mary Flores (pictured in costume) and other Texon invitees attended a masquerade ball in Best. In December of that year, BLOC employees formed an orchestra, the Reagan County Singing Group performed popular oldies, and by January 1932, the church sponsored a singing school. Ladies from Texon, Best, and Santa Rita formed bridge clubs, and dinner and ice cream parties were common. In February 1931, a talent show netted the Red Cross $70.75. By late 1925, Texon Masons, including H.L. "Bob" Adams, had joined Big Lake Lodge No. 1203, whose building was financed in part by Levi Smith. Texon women like Maude Shepard affiliated with Big Lake's Eastern Star chapter. In January 1930, John Stewart of Texon was a San Angelo DeMolay initiate. (John de la Garza.)

Organized in January 1927 and church-sponsored, Boy Scout Troop 55, Concho Valley Council, became a positive community influence. Charter members included James Bennett, Noble Fisk, Donald Graham, James Hill, Wishart McCarty, Adrian Pearce, and Aubrey White. Succeeding first Scoutmaster David Coulter were Rev. W.E. Sampson and Paul Burton. Scouts attended camps at Menard, Carlsbad, and Fort Stockton before the 1929 creation of Camp Louis Farr (above), the designated council camp in adjoining Irion County. The troop, at a Court of Honor in the Texon Clubhouse, received its charter on July 14, 1931. Council members present, such as Texon Store operator Rudolph Theis and Scout executive B.W. Draper, praised the troop's fine record. Parents and other supportive Texon adults expressed pride. Pictured below is the Scout collection of E.P. Bennett. (Above, Ettawah Cagle Morris; below, JSW.)

This panoramic picture, taken from the air in 1928, shows Texas Street, which was considered Texon's "main street," to the south (left) of the Orient tracks. The light-colored roofs on the houses along Texas Street are the company boardinghouse and the Texon Café. The Texon Theatre and the ballpark are located behind Texas Street. To the left of the ballpark is the hospital. The road in front of the hospital runs out of the photograph to the picnic grounds and Colina Alta

Golf Course. Located north (right) of the railroad tracks, Santa Rita No. 1's wooden derrick is distinguishable from BLOC's shops and warehouses. The gasoline plant, which skimmed gas from the crude oil and sent it to refineries, is at the upper right. Most of the Big Lake Field is to the right and out of the picture. (Riley Spraggins.)

This 1926 shotgun house is an example of the earliest type of company-built framed housing. Families eventually moved to more spacious dwellings, although some shotguns were occupied for several years. Shade trees, which the BLOC planted in 1929, and shrubs and grass combated high temperatures and incessant wind and dust. Latticed vines frequently shaded western exposures, as pictured. All family residences had porches, which along with commonplace swings encouraged outside evening socializing as nighttime cooling set in. Company maintenance men made repairs, painted, and did remodeling. The average home had four rooms and a utility room in the rear that later converted to a bathroom. In the first years, rent was assessed at $1 per room per month. (Photographs by BT.)

Two

THE GOOD YEARS

From 1932 to the end of World War II, Texon experienced both stability and change. Big Lake Oil Company vice president and general manager Charles E. Beyer pushed forward with deep drilling. Until his retirement in 1943, Ted Williams maintained close involvement in, and oversight of, the day-to-day affairs. Established institutions—namely the school, church, and hospital—continued to be vital and appreciated. Flourishing social organizations and inexpensive, people-generated recreational activities had wide appeal. These organizations also reinforced a growing sense of community, a family-like feeling in this isolated, self-contained setting.

Although it might seem ironic to later generations, in many ways Texon's best years were those of the Great Depression. Its quality of life and relative prosperity were out of the mainstream during those hard times. The town's housewives gave food to those who "rode the rails," and telegrapher Margaret Dixon remembered hoboes spending the night in the Santa Fe depot. Then there was the Jewel Schaible family. They operated the dairy and at one point in the mid-1930s decided to pull up stakes and return to their native Arkansas. Once there, however, they found conditions so dire, recalled wife, Louvena, that "we didn't waste much time getting back" to Texon.

As Texon hummed along, three factors pointed to change and provided an indication of things to come. Despite continued drilling, the Big Lake Field's annual output declined from 6,535,000 barrels in 1933 to 1,407,000 in 1945. That year marked an end to 36 months of "dry holes" and caused Beyer to admit, "Our future prospects are limited to our present producing wells." Earlier, in 1934, Plymouth Oil, BLOC's parent, tapped productive leases near Sinton, in coastal San Patricio County, and completed the first well of the Olson Field in Crockett County. Plymouth transferred experienced field and office personnel from Texon to both new operations. Finally, the war had a telling affect. Many of the prewar employees who entered the armed services, as well as the young men who enlisted out of high school, took advantage of the GI Bill's educational benefits and did not return. Those who took high-paying jobs in the defense industry or those, especially young women, who left for employment opportunities and training in Texas cities and other states were also among the members of the community who did not return after the war. The town's population, which peaked at about 1,150 in 1930, was approximately 740 in 1945.

Texon was going to be different.

Levi Smith's death placed Charles E. Beyer in charge. Born in St. Louis in 1885, he studied geology at the University of California, Los Angeles, and went to work in Mexico's oil fields. Here, in 1914, he met Smith and signed on with him at B-T's Penn-Mex operation. He then returned to California as head of Santa Barbara Oil, another B-T holding. In 1925, he spent a few months with Smith in Texon, and four years later, he located there permanently as BLOC's general manager. His wife and two children never lived in Texon. He succeeded Smith—whom he affectionately called *jefe* (chief)—not as company president but as vice president and thus with less clout. Although lacking Smith's personal touch, Beyer, pictured above in 1934, continued his old friend's policies and won the respect of the employees as an able administrator. (LBC Collection, Petroleum Museum.)

Englishman James S. Posgate, BLOC assistant general manager under both Levi Smith and Charles Beyer, worked in Milwaukee, Dallas, and Kansas before joining British-owned Mexican Eagle Oil Company as pipeline and construction superintendent. In Mexico, he met Smith, and in 1929, Posgate, his wife, Emily, and Kansas-born son Jimmy arrived in Texon. A daily routine of afternoon tea added a unique flavor to Texon life. Emily accompanied Girl Scout carolers on her grand piano and served them hot chocolate. She was an active member of the Myrtle Pearce Bible Study Club. Posgate, who rode his horse regularly and played with the polo team, retired to California in 1937. (Photograph by BT.)

The early wells tapped the shallow Permian strata but soon gave way to the deeper Ordovician-level, or "C" series, wells of the 1930s. Several of them exceeded 9,000 feet, and in December 1932, BLOC owned six of the world's 12 deepest wells. In 1933, mule teams were still in use. Here, they are shown dragging the steel derrick for a deep C well. (Photograph by BT.)

This C series well is spewing wet gas under high pressure. By the end of 1941—the Big Lake Field's 18th year—its production was 78,877,610 barrels, or approximately 5.25 percent of the Permian Basin output for the same period. It contributed almost seven percent of the Basin's West Texas yield from 21 counties. (Photograph by BT.)

The deeper drilling expanded the Big Lake Field. After 15 years, by August 1938, BLOC had paid $1,265,000 in county, school, and state taxes, contributed $10,500,000 in royalties to the University of Texas, and maintained a payroll that amounted to $7,555,000. The four BLOC employees pictured by a C well are, from left to right, Howard Bushager, Claude Bosworth, Mickey McDonald, and Monte Bosworth. (Mai Bosworth Hamilton.)

Pumpers who regularly checked working wells and other BLF workers stayed in "dog houses" while not making their rounds. These small buildings provided protection against severe temperatures and blowing dust and a place to complete daily records. (Photograph by James A. Wilson.)

Along with traditional office duties, BLOC's all-male office staff, many with college or business school backgrounds, had town-related responsibilities. They managed the hospital, theater, and Oilers accounts and collected rent and electricity payments. They also compiled monthly field production reports for the Texas Railroad Commission. In early years, the manually operated, 24-hour PBX telephone switchboard was in the office. Pictured in 1928 are, front desk M.E. Whiteside; middle desk Jim Isbell, right, and Hal Burton; back desk Barron McCulloch, right, George Raphael, middle, unidentified, and Homer Young; standing, John Huffman.

Many office personnel stayed until retirement or transfer. The 1934 staff members pictured above are, from left to right, Jim Isbell, Homer Young, Paul Burton, Arthur Flores, Hal Burton, unidentified, Jesse Thompson, and unidentified. Pictured below, staff members from the late 1930s are, from left to right, (first row) Harrie Smith, Harvey Dunlap, Osa Goble, Paul Crews, and Homer Young; (second row) Thornton Stewart, W.F. Grissett, Jim Isbell, Jack Hitt, and Clint Johnson. (Above, Arthur Flores; below, photograph by BT.)

In the early 1900s, M.R. "Ted" Williams, a St. Louis native born in 1878, entered the oil business in Beaumont's Spindletop Field, whose discovery marked a new petroleum age. In revolutionary Mexico, he worked for English-owned Mexican Eagle Oil, met Levi Smith, and in 1914, joined B-T's Penn-Mex. B-T then sent him to Colombia, and in 1923, he was appointed assistant secretary for BLOC. He figured in the planning of Texon, and while serving as de facto mayor and city manager, his many responsibilities included the clubhouse, tennis courts, theater, and school prior to joining the county district. He also helped organize the company's Christmas gift giving. Children saw him as a benevolent tyrant who insisted upon proper public conduct, especially in the theater. Williams is pictured in 1934 with his dog Popeye, the Oilers' unofficial mascot. (Wallace Carnes.)

44

Halamicek Brothers purchased what residents called the "grocery store," and Paul Halamicek managed it throughout the 1930s. Although specials were offered in 1934 on Fridays and Saturdays, prices reflected Texon's isolation and were slightly higher than in Big Lake, which prompted the Halamicek circular pictured at right. When completed in the mid-1930s, the paving of Highway 67 encouraged groups of housewives to shop in San Angelo. Goods like those pictured below were no problem, but vegetables suffered from the lack of refrigeration. In early 1933, the New Deal's bank holiday briefly halted money transactions in favor of chits. When banks reopened, Halamicek Brothers, in the weekly *Big Lake Wildcat*, praised the honesty of its Texon customers. In 1943, Herbert Bernshausen, Paul's nephew, bought the store. In November 1944, his newspaper advertisement encouraged people to "save paper" by using shopping bags. (Right, cartoon by Jesse Thompson; below, photograph by BT.)

"Believe It Or Not" but—
We wish to add to Ripley's —
the fact that:

If you buy groceries, etc., 15 miles from here add $2.50 to your bill irrespective of the size of the purchase, In other words, a 15¢ can of beans costs you $2.65 — —
Why?
It actually costs you 7½¢ a mile to operate your automobile — in this country — —
It's Cheaper To Buy In Texon!

The Texon Café, a natural adult gathering place, served consistently good food and, after the repeal of Prohibition in 1933, cold beer. It hosted bridge clubs and banquets for golfers, school trustees, teachers, and high school groups. In 1931, when J.W. Juergens assumed management, both kitchen offerings and service suffered, and diners patronized Abe Gross's café in Santa Rita, the nearby Texon Land and Oil Company camp. "Mom" and "Dad" Wright took over, restored traditional quality, and stayed until 1940. During World War II, Gross, A.D. "Fats" and Claudia Adams, and Elson and Mae Shattuck operated the café. The Christmas theme seen in the photograph above greeted BLOC employees at the counter. They are, from left to right, Vonnie Brown, R.R. "Cotton" Kerlin, Earl "Hardwood" Brooks, L.B. "Blondy" Menielle, Hal Burton, and two unidentified. (Photograph by BT.)

Expert BEAUTY Work

PERMANENT WAVES - $1.95 to $5.00

SHAMPOOING, FINGERWAVING,

MANICURING, MARCELLING

AND OTHER BEAUTY WORK

MRS. GREGG'S

HOME BEAUTY SHOP
— Texon Texas —

In 1935, Mollie Jordan operated the beauty shop, and Bertha McLeod took over in 1937. Lola Gregg's flyer shown above advertised one of several in-home shops. When Aris Thorp, owner of the barbershop and tailor shop, died in 1935, his wife leased both shop spaces. The Thorps had employed Grover Weaver and Lacy Way in the tailor shop, and Way operated it from 1936 to 1940. In 1940, Oscar Lee bought the barbershop and tailor shop, and in 1942, he sold it to J.J. Campbell, who also acquired the beauty shop. In the late 1930s, Ozona Laundry picked up washables left at the tailor shop three days a week, though that was reduced to two days during the war because of gas and rubber rationing. (Jesse Thompson.)

Fred Garver, the first Santa Fe depot agent, remained until 1936, when L.C. Ochsner replaced him and stayed until October 1943. J.H. Hamilton served until July 1945, succeeded by O.B. Poole. The World War II Doodlebug and depot were much in demand by armed services personnel and civilians hampered by wartime automotive shortages. The depot on Texas Street, located next to Santa Rita No. 1, is pictured above in 1934. Garver and Ochsner were ham radio operators, and they and other Texon "hams" provided valuable service in emergency situations. Garver's station was W5AVY. Ochsner's was W5Dga, as noted on the 1936 ham postcard below. (Above, photograph by BT; below, JSW.)

Alma McGonagle's ownership of Texon Drug continued through the early 1930s. She hired pharmacist Tom Beverly in 1933 and, in 1935, sold the store to Mr. and Mrs. A.P. "Doc" Simpson. In 1941, pharmacist R.E. "Red" Rogers, pictured, became owner. After acquiring the store, Rogers soon married Texon Hospital nurse Jerry Dillon, who was the store's manager while Rogers was in the Navy. Wartime pharmacists were C.C. Anglin and L.E. Lunsford. The drugstore regularly employed teenagers, including Weaver Pool, Neal Shepard, Maxine Adams, Marion Lee Spraggins, and Bette Goble. (Maxine Adams Hyden.)

Pictured is J. Edgar "Las Vegas Kim" Kimsey, a cowboy artist and former rodeo bull rider who was postmaster from 1929 until his resignation in 1941. During his tenure, the Depression-era chain letter craze captivated the nation and Texon. In late 1941, William M. "Mack" Irby succeeded Kimsey and began a long-term service. During World War II, the post office took on added importance for those awaiting word from loved ones in uniform. It was where townspeople exchanged news and where war savings stamps and bonds were purchased. Postal clerks included Kimsey's wife, Lurlyne, Paul Crews, and Norma Irby. (JSW.)

49

In September 1931, W.L. "Bill" Thompson and Rodney Pearce resigned their BLOC positions to travel to New York City to attend a course, sponsored by the Radio Corporation of America (RCA), on the installation and servicing of theater sound equipment. In November 1932, Thompson and Glen Byars opened the Texon Photo and Radio Shop next to the grocery store. They provided film processing, photograph enlargement, and radio repair. Byars soon left town, and BLOC rehired Thompson, who expanded the business to include rental and installation of public address systems, which found demand from rodeos and sporting events, including Oilers games. Tony Slaughter, a former Texon resident and San Angelo sports writer, announced for Thompson and is shown here. (Photograph by BT.)

While in New York, Bill Thompson and Rodney Pearce visited radio network studios. Back in Texon, Thompson created station WHOA early in 1933. This was his public address system, with microphones in the drugstore and wired speakers set up behind the building. Weekly broadcasts featured local and area talent. Youthful Wichert McCarty provided guitar accompaniment for his Western songs, Santa Fe agent Fred Garver gave literary readings, and musician-comedian Lewis Slaughter (pictured) orated as "Senator Stormy Weather." Jesse Thompson and Pearce were announcers. The free broadcasts drew sizeable crowds and competed with the Texon Theatre to the extent that manager Ted Williams asked, and Thompson agreed, to relocate the production to the theater. By April 1933, theater broadcasts complimented feature films. (Photograph by BT.)

The Texon Red Peppers were regulars on WHOA. Seated are guitarist George Scott and banjo player Tom Baldridge, and standing on the left is an unidentified person alongside fiddler Orval McCaa. Other performers not pictured included steel guitarist Homer Bridges and Mr. and Mrs. H. Ford Taylor of Big Lake, who offered "songs you'll like to hear." (Photograph by BT.)

WHOA shows also featured the piano duo of Christine (Johnson) and Tony Slaughter, who played the latest popular tunes. In May 1933, after its move to the Texon Theatre, WHOA presented its hour-long *Amalgamated Buggy Whip Program*, a live broadcast over Radio Station KGKL, San Angelo. (Photograph by BT.)

Texon Theatre

ROXY ENTERTAINMENT · · · · · · · · · · · · · · · · · · · AT TEXON PRICES

FRIDAY SATURDAY
November 24-25

SPECIAL
SATURDAY
NIGHT ONLY

Broadcast to begin
about 9:30

COMING
Sun., Dec. 10

THE BOWERY

SHANGHAI MADNESS

With Spencer Tracy and Fay Wray and
Our usual interesting and educational short reels.

Radio Broadcast

From Station P-U-N-K, on our stage

6————————BIG ACTS————————6

1......TOM & GEORGE
BANJO AND GUITAR HARMONY

2......NEAL SHEPARD
"HOT-FOOT" HIMSELF

3......JAMES ALLISON
BING CROSBY'S RIVAL

4.....SENATOR STORMY WEATHER
A FAIRY TALE FOR THE KIDDIES

5......WISHERT M'CARTY
THE KGKL BLUES YODELER

6......MRS. DYKE FULLER
"STEP LIVELY" (PIANO)

SUNDAY-MONDAY | **BROADWAY TO HOLLYWOOD**

TUESDAY | Ever in My Heart
FAMILY NIGHT, 10c- 20c

Wed.-Thurs.-Fri.
MATINEE

Thanksgiving Afternoon . 10c-25c

MAE WEST
IN HER VERY LATEST SENSATION
I'M NO ANGEL

1933

In late November 1933, following a glowing write-up in the *San Angelo Morning Times*, six WHOA acts appeared on the Texon Theatre stage on the bill with Spencer Tracy and Fay Wray in *Shanghai Madness* and several short features. The ticket prices for the show were 25¢ for adults and 10¢ for children. The WHOA performances were part of a nationwide trend of giving Great Depression moviegoers more for the price of a ticket in order to keep seats filled. Manager Ted Williams added cash and merchandise drawings and baby and beauty contests, and he showcased local talent. The theater, as this flyer touts, strove to provide "Roxy Entertainment" at "Texon Prices." (Jesse Thompson.)

The theater was central to life in Texon. The picture show represented culture, education, entertainment, and socializing—something for everyone. Its ticket prices undercut the mid-1930s national average of 27¢, and its "sound and screen equipment," as remembered by Bill Thompson, equaled "any in Texas." The theater offered the following: the majority of Hollywood's best films, from gangsters to ghouls; Tom Mix, Gene Autry, and Red Rider serials; and *Pathé News* and *March of Time*. *Texon Topics*, Arthur Flores's hour-long film depicting the town's everyday life, was popular. There were band concerts, cash and dish giveaways, a horse race money game, the "Lonesome Cowboy" singer from powerful border station XER, and renowned operatic baritone Joseph Burger. Young men in the theater's poster frame are, from left to right, John Stewart, Jesse Thompson, and Rodney Pearce. (Photograph by BT.)

In 1932, Johnny and Era Flynn arrived in town and worked in the theater throughout its existence. Era sold tickets, and Johnny assisted Ted Williams, who succeeded Ben Donaldson at the projector. Williams trained several young men to operate the projector, including Mike Adams and Marion Spraggins. Marion and brother R.W. made popcorn and earned 1¢ per bag sold. Others, like June Barbee and Babe Bennett, received movie passes for various chores. War in Europe and Pearl Harbor brought anti-Axis films, and the patriotic Williams made sure youngsters stayed put during newsreels. His 1943 retirement ended his 20-year, hands-on dedication to Texon. Pictured is Mary Frances Sutton, and behind her is the theater's billboard, spotlighting Cary Grant in Alfred Hitchcock's psychothriller *Suspicion* (1941). (R.W. Spraggins.)

Dynamic pastor Dr. A.E. Arnfield and the Texon Union Church council launched a vigorous membership drive, retired the classroom debt, and created a Sunday school class for every family member. For December 1934, church and Sunday school attendance reached 975. In October 1932, Arnfield continued the tradition of annual revivals, and the church frequently hosted the Permian Basin Singing Convention and continued its sponsorship of the Boy Scouts. Sunday school and Bible classes and the Young People's Society were responsible for evening services. The church pulsated with activity under Arnfield, who resigned in late 1935, the last of the company-paid ministers. The stag parties and barbecues for the men's Bible class, pictured, encouraged church membership and supported various community activities. At far left is Levi Smith, behind Arnfield. (John R. Daugherty.)

The women's Sunday school classes, the LWT and Fidelis, were vital to the church. Their monthly programs were part of the services, and they purchased a new piano, drapes for the altar, and a communion table. Their clubhouse socials were open to all Texon women, their basketball teams competed against local and area teams, and they raised funds to purchase letter sweaters for the Reagan County High School girls' basketball team. Pictured is the LWT class in the mid-1930s. Mrs. A.E. Arnfield is in the first row, tenth from the left. (LBC.)

In the late 1930s and early 1940s, area clergymen and lay members led services on Sunday and Wednesday evenings, and baptisms were held at the swimming pool. The annual "White Christmas" tradition continued, in which each member of the congregation placed food items wrapped in white under the Christmas tree. They were given to a needy Big Lake family. Music remained important, and the junior a cappella choir, pictured above, often sang. Director Irene Teele is in the third row on the far right. Soloists were (first row) Guy Eddie Bosworth, far left, and Johnny Mack Garrison, third from left, and (second row) Jack Moore, second from right. Piano accompanist Marilyn Moore is located in the fourth row, on the far left. The church's south side, pictured below, included its member-funded classroom on the far left. (Above, Irene Teele; below, JSW.)

Several doctors served the Texon Hospital during the 1930s and early 1940s. C.W. Ory left in February 1933, succeeded by P.M. Waltrip (1933–1935), Thomas Carbrey (1935–1937), and W.F. Birdsong (1937–1941). Pictured at left, with his wife, Atrelle, is Charles "Choc" McCollum, the dentist, anesthesiologist, and dispenser of good humor for hospitalized patients. He moved to Odessa in 1940. Wartime doctors were Carbrey (1941–1943), Glen T. Pearson (1943–1944) pictured below with son, and H.C. Samuels (1944–1945). They treated oil field–related injuries, childhood diseases, and anything else that came their way. Before penicillin became available, they feared peritonitis and performed a large number of appendectomies. (Left, LBC; below, Dr. Glen Pearson.)

Both registered and licensed vocational nurses worked at the Texon Hospital and did whatever was assigned to them. They assisted in surgery, dispensed medications, looked after and consoled patients, and administered first aid. Nearly half of those who served from 1933 to 1945 married while in Texon. Pictured above is Velma Spivey, who joined the hospital staff in 1943, with her husband, Orba "Sonny" Harvey, a BLOC employee. The company paid the nurses' salaries and provided living quarters: a four-bedroom, two-bath house, pictured below, for single women. Nurses took their meals in the hospital kitchen. (Both, Velma Spivey Harvey.)

Nurse Mary Swift is pictured at left with Iris and Elizabeth Davis and holding her daughter Mary Kay. Swift arrived in Texon from Comfort, Texas, in 1939. She became the wife of Paul Carroll, a teacher in the Texon School. Recently discharged from the Women's Army Corps (WAC), Paula McLeod came to Texon in 1945 and was hired as a nurse's aide. She is pictured below, in later years, with Texon-born Leonard Bird, a BLOC employee, whom she married in 1948. (Left, Bob Talley; below, photograph by James A. Wilson.)

Texon boys took to Scouting. From 1933 to 1945, Troop 55 Scoutmasters were Hal Burton, Foy White, J.B. Morris, and Leonard Lee. Rev. A.E. Arnfield, H.L. "Bob" Adams, and L.B. Menielle were other stalwarts. Activities included outings at Camp Louis Farr, swimming meets with other troops, and "camporees" with area Scouts. Scouts working on merit badges and advanced ranks performed community service. At regularly held Tri-City Courts of Honor, troop members from Iraan, McCamey, and Rankin were presented their badges. During this period, at least a dozen boys achieved Eagle Scout status. In 1935, Eagle Scouts Stuart Conley and Dan and John R. Daugherty, along with Rector McCollum, went on the Concho Valley Council's 4,000-mile Rocky Mountain Tour. Pictured are Scoutmaster Leonard Lee and an unidentified Scout at Camp Louis Farr. (JSW.)

In 1937, a community effort built the Scout House. Dallas contractor W. Lee Morris, father of Scoutmaster J.B. Morris, designed the log-style building with a rock fireplace, cement floor, and shuttered windows. Rig builders, Scouts, and their fathers, supervised by contractor Morris, provided the labor. BLOC contributed bricks, power poles for logs, and roofing lumber. General manager Charles Beyer personally paid for the fireplace, which was built by company employee John McClelland's father. Ted Williams gave decorative animal skins, and Bob Adams made furniture. On October 8, 1937, a Court of Honor and barbecue dedicated the Scout House. Pictured above is construction of the house; the fireplace is below. (Both, JSW.)

Scouts gave their all to the war effort. In the prewar summer of 1941, they conducted a house-to-house aluminum drive and began collecting paper. That same year, the Boy Scouts of America undertook a scrap iron drive that saw Troop 55 gather 105,400 pounds. In October 1942, the boys won praise in a letter, published in newspapers, from the wife of a crane operator at an Ohio steel mill. When the freight car with Texon scrap arrived, she wrote, "The cheers went up. You did a grand job." In 1944, scouts planted a Victory Garden and filled a truck with three tons of paper for delivery to the Army Air Corps' Goodfellow Field in San Angelo. By June 1945, they had sold more than $25,000 in war bonds. (LBC.)

Members of Troop 55 pose atop a New York Central freight car loaded with their collection of scrap iron bound for an Ohio rolling mill. Scouts are, from left to right, two unidentified, Butch Kelly, unidentified, Bobby Joe Warren, Billy Keene, Hollis Marshall, unidentified, Edward Smelser, Pat Shattuck, Charles Rogers, Burke Isbell, Jackie Stewart, and Harrie A. Smith. Shown below are, from left to right, Jeff Kelly, Charles Beyer, unidentified, Tom Reed, and Kate Maris. (LBC.)

Levi Smith's gift giving to children under 12, along with $10 employee bonuses, continued at the company's expense under BLOC president J.G. Farquhar. In 1933, the company's Christmas tree was in the theater, then it was in the "Barn" from 1934 through 1941, when carols blended with post–Pearl Harbor patriotic songs. During the Depression of the 1930s, a company present made the difference in a child's Christmas, and Pearl Oldham believed that youngsters got "better gifts each year." In 1942, A.D. "Fats" Adams was Santa, and Ted Williams presided at the theater, where, for the next two years, Johnny and Era Flynn took charge and jovial C.C. Sandy donned the beard and red suit. Charles Beyer reflected the following in his newsletter to servicemen: the "contagious joy of the little ones" overshadowed "our trials and tribulations." (Fay Grissett.)

The Texon Oilers were winners. In 1933 and 1934, they captured the West Texas League title. The 1934 club won the two-league West Texas regional championship and took two games from a previously undefeated House of David team. The 1935 Oilers, pictured, won a 14-inning thriller over Ozona for the Permian Basin League crown. Pitching from Flop Harris, Hi Haven, and Wally Ritter, was strong; infielders Trigg Housewright, Putsy Gentry, Gus Leedy, and Roy Gardner, routinely turned double plays; and the team batting average was above .280, which included Eddie "Watermelon" McMillan's league-leading .419. As competition improved, the 1936 and 1937 seasons were good but subpar. In 1938, the Oilers rallied to compile a winning record, and in 1939, the team rallied and was the Permian Basin League champion once again. (BT.)

New names like Joe Kosel, Frank "Lefty" Jacot, and Jack Brown began to appear on the Oilers roster alongside such mainstays as manager Snipe Conley, the ever-dependable catcher Curtis "Iron Man" Barbee, and pitching stalwart Archie Peel. The team played as an independent in 1940, the same year it lost to the American League St. Louis Browns, 9-2, in a game to benefit the construction of San Angelo's community gymnasium. By 1941, players were aging; Plymouth, BLOC's parent company, had transferred some; and fewer competitive area teams resulted in a scaled-down schedule. Then, World War II postponed semiprofessional baseball. It also marked the end of the Oilers the people of Texon had come to cherish. Nevertheless, the Oilers heritage endured. Pictured in 1934 is first baseman Roy Gardner. (Mr. and Mrs. Roy Gardner Collection, Petroleum Museum.)

The Texon School, part of the Reagan County Independent School District, housed grades one through seven until 1940, when, under the state's 6-6 (or 12-year) plan, seventh graders transferred to Big Lake. In the 1930s and early 1940s, BLOC employee Roy Pearce was a member, then president, of the county school board. Above are Texon teachers in 1933. Those pictured are, from left to right, (first row) principal E.W. LeFevre, Geneva Duderstadt, Lilla Hickerson, Mary Lauren Pierce, and Paul Carroll; (second row) Ruby McCollum, Helen Elrod, Irene Teele, Mary Fawn Coulter, and Norine Maxey. Until the war years, the principal's nine-month salary was $1,980. Teachers earned $1,200. For the 1945–1946 school year, some teachers' pay was raised to $1,673. (JSW.)

BLOC provided living quarters for single women in the teacherage on Texas Street, pictured above. Each bedroom accommodated two teachers, and hot plates were provided, although eating out was normal. For many, summers meant graduate studies or working toward undergraduate degrees, since some taught with temporary certificates. Teacher involvement in the community, especially the church, was expected, and in the early years, the school board preferred that females not marry. Pictured below in the teacherage are Marie Rhodes, standing, with Ruby McCollum seated to her right and Bessie Chyle Leath seated to McCollum's left. The two women in front are unidentified. (Above, Burke Isbell; below, Ettawah Cagle Morris.)

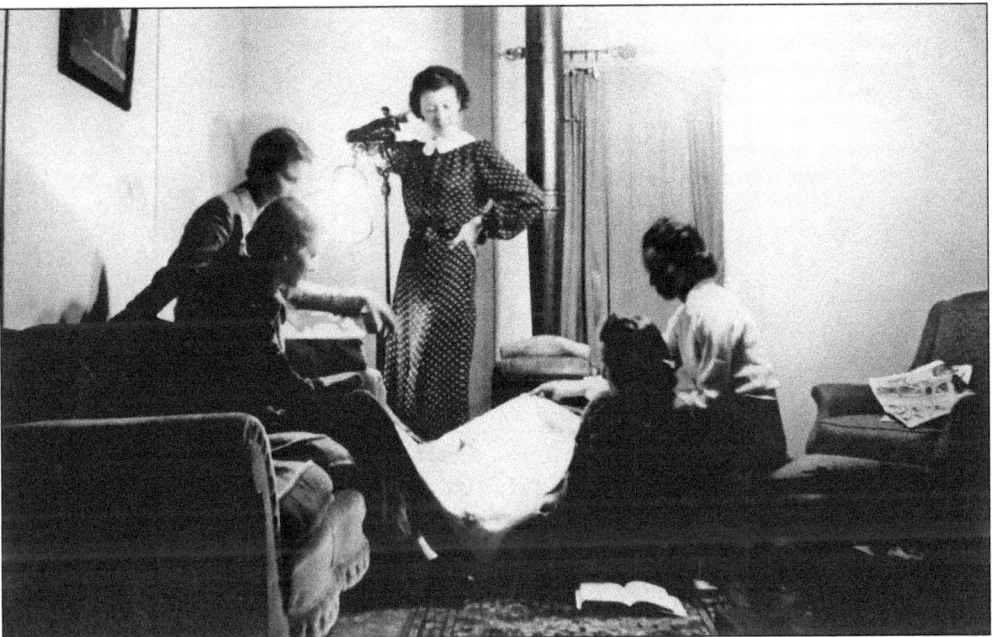

Teacher Norine Maxey's 1932–1933 first-grade pupils are, from left to right, (first row) Junior Archie, Corrine Satterfield, Gene Cook, Jack Shepard, Margaret Johnson, Mary Jane Spraggins, unidentified, Joan Huffman, Jim Newbrough, Lloyd Shattuck, Margie Everhart, Buddy Criswell, and unidentified; (second row) Betty Grace Garrison, Betty Shattuck, John Arledge, Buddy Carnes, unidentified, Monroe Satterfield, Charles Griffith, Don Warriner, Maxine Adams, unidentified, Mary Jean Sawyer, and unidentified. (JSW.)

These 1932–1933 sixth-graders of Irene Teele, center of second row, graduated from Texon School at a ceremony in 1934, at which C.E. Carter and Rector McCollum were valedictorian and salutatorian, Ruth Mildred Gambill gave the class history, and Joe Talley played a violin solo. Those pictured are, from left to right, (first row) unidentified, Macie Garrison, Jack Garver, Rector McCollum, C.E. Carter, two unidentified, Joe Talley, and four unidentified; (second row) unidentified, Bernice Harris, unidentified, Veda Fell, Ruth Mildred Gambill, unidentified, Buddy Whitney, two unidentified, and Glyndon Bowen. (Irene Teele.)

This 1939–1940 sixth-grade class of Marie McCollum included Harmonica Band members in distinctive headgear. Those pictured are, from right to left, (first row) Madeline ?, Bette Goble, Pete Allen, and Buddy Carnes; (second row) Sidney Brown, Tommy Slatton, Maxine Brown, Jim Newbrough, Bobby Newbrough, and Clarice Johnson; (third row) Clayburn Bird, Virginia Leedy, unidentified, Mary Frances Downing, Bobbie Lou Graves, Betty Grace Garrison, Maxine Adams, and Mary Frances Goeppinger. (Maxine Adams Hyden.)

Texon was important to Reagan County High School (RCHS) in Big Lake. Texon parents were leaders in the school's Parent Teacher Association (PTA), and, in 1933, BLOC provided a field for the RCHS Owls football team to use as a neutral site. Ellen Jane Bennett was one of several Texon members of the girls' basketball team. Participation in University Interscholastic League competition, such as band and debate, allowed Texon youth to shine. During 1942–1943, a six-day school week and an early commencement freed students for ranch work or enlistment. Wartime also meant curtailment of some extracurricular activities. This 1942 photograph shows Texon girls in front of RCHS. They are, from left to right, (first row) Bobbie Lou Graves and Maxine Adams; (second row) Jane Spraggins, Joan Gooch, Bette Goble, and Corrine Satterfield. (JSW.)

Irene Potter, later Mrs. Oliver Teele, arrived in 1928 to teach music in the Texon School. She organized a rhythm band—bells, sticks, tambourines, and triangles—for the primary grades. For grades five through seven, she created a harmonica and accordion band that was always called "the Harmonica Band." It also included guitars and xylophones, and several band members were tap dancers and vocalists. The accordion and harmonica were popular during the 1930s, and during the Depression the harmonica was affordable. The band performed at the Texon Theatre and area schools, and every spring it was broadcast over San Angelo's Radio Station KGKL. It won second place at the Federation of Music Clubs competition in San Angelo, and in 1934, took first at a similar event in San Antonio. This win qualified the band for the national meet in Minneapolis, which they were unable to attend. Through the years, Teele and the students' mothers designed and made band uniforms. She retired in 1940, the Harmonica Band's last year. (Courtesy Irene Teele, JSW.)

Students rode buses 14 miles from Texon, with stops in Santa Rita and Best, to RCHS. The 1930s buses pictured above served until 1941 when the new bus, below, replaced them. It seated 100 or more, was reputed to be the nation's largest bus, and might have been one of the popular Chevrolet/Wayne models. Painted blue and gold, the school colors, it defied the prevailing all-yellow standard. In the early 1940s, teacher Gladys Trantham was the all-seeing bus monitor. (Above, Gwen Goble Rivers; below, Gert Satterfield Doak.)

Texon's Labor Day celebration continued from 1933 through 1941. During that time, R.J. Cook, of Ozona, barbecued the beef. As before, festivities varied and included an Oilers game and field events such as throwing, base running, trap shooting, golf matches, and a boxing card. Special movies were shown, like Charlie Chaplin's *Modern Times* (1936) and *Slim* with Pat O'Brien (1937). A concluding dance may have featured the touring Joe Teagarden Band (1933) or the Kenneth Allen Orchestra (1934) and Harrison Texans (1936), both of San Angelo. In 1935, when some 1,600 ate free barbecue, James S. Posgate, BLOC's assistant general manager, distributed some 500 pounds of surplus meat to the area's needy. Wartime celebrations held in 1944 and 1945 featured barbecued ham and cheese sandwiches and chicken. Pictured is the 1936 program cover. (David Werst.)

While visiting in early 1933, BLOC board chairman Joe Trees commented that Texon—which was otherwise perfect—needed a swimming pool. That summer, the company's construction crew, with the help of hired high school and college boys, dug and blasted a hole on Golf Hill. Because cement pouring occurred at night, car headlights illuminated the construction site. On September 17, the J.C. Trees Pool, complete with a lifeguard stand, steps on the shallow end, metal ladders in the middle, and a diving board at the deep end, opened to a capacity crowd of youngsters, who, according to one resident, had "gone daffy" over the new facility. Near the pool were showers and dressing rooms, as well as a clubhouse with a porch and chairs for mothers with small children. Pictured above is Hal Burton, and below is the pool's commemorative plaque. (Above, Arthur Flores; below, photograph by Wesley Daugherty.)

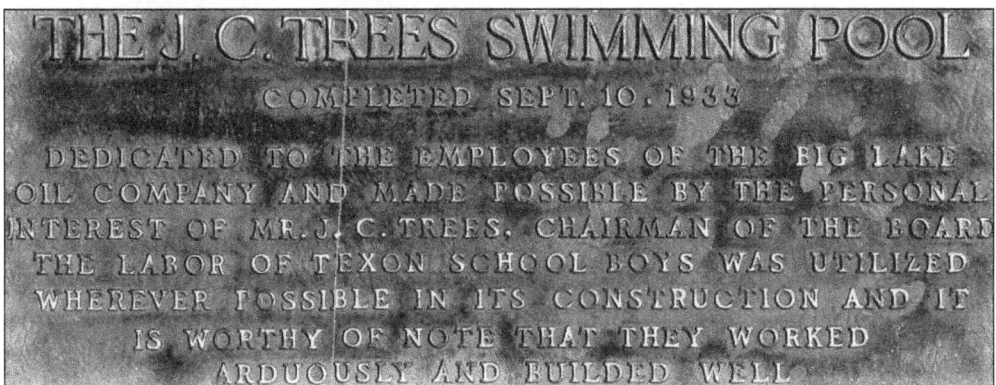

THE J. C. TREES SWIMMING POOL
COMPLETED SEPT. 10, 1933

DEDICATED TO THE EMPLOYEES OF THE BIG LAKE
OIL COMPANY AND MADE POSSIBLE BY THE PERSONAL
INTEREST OF MR. J. C. TREES, CHAIRMAN OF THE BOARD
THE LABOR OF TEXON SCHOOL BOYS WAS UTILIZED
WHEREVER POSSIBLE IN ITS CONSTRUCTION AND IT
IS WORTHY OF NOTE THAT THEY WORKED
ARDUOUSLY AND BUILDED WELL

Texon's two asphalt-surfaced tennis courts hosted young beginners and accomplished players. And more than a few teachers took up racquets. Pictured are teacher Ruby McCollum, left, and Maude Shepard. Croquet also caught on as early as 1932, and the courts, located between the post office and the theater, were owned by Alton Stinson and had lights for night play. By 1934, a croquet club was being discussed. In 1935, twelve local two-man teams were doing battle, and another court was being prepared. Players included A.A. Criswell, Troy Gambill, Freck Seifert, Hiram Smelser, and Bill Spraggins. Marble players also "knuckled down" with their favorite "taws" (shooters) on the croquet courts' tamped down surface. A privately owned pool hall, domino parlor, and bowling alley operated briefly. (Ettawah Cagle Morris.)

Golf's appeal remained strong. The Colina Alta course underwent considerable changes in 1934, including new oiled sand greens, which were common in West Texas. One of them is pictured above. Seasoned players like Jim Isbell, left-handed Bob and brother Pat Kelly, and Jack Satterwhite did well in area tournaments. Texon entered a team in the Kat Klaw League in 1935, when Alta Colina's fairways, as pictured below, boasted "more grass" than "any other" league course. By the early 1940s, a new generation of names, including Oliver "Boob" Howard, Jack Moore, and Bill Mac Varnadore, appeared on the golf ladder. The 1941 invitational tournament, with a $2 entry fee, was hotly contested on greens refurbished through the generosity of Charles Beyer and field superintendent Clint Johnson. (Above, photograph by BT; below, Vonnie Brown.)

DRIVE AROUND FAIRWAY →

Texon residents took to a variety of sports, including a brief fascination with the new game of speedball. Early 1934 witnessed formation of a Texon Athletic Club. Teams like the Engineers, Pipeliners, Roustabouts, and Office Force represented company departments in volleyball and baseball, both outdoor and in BLOC's Big Barn-turned-gymnasium. A men's basketball team played teams from the surrounding area. Following the Oilers season, "softball fever" produced colorfully named teams like teacher Paul "Squatcho" Carroll's "Squatchorinos." The athletic club's women's division organized basketball and volleyball teams that played each other and out-of-town teams. Boxing was another activity that filled the company's white-roofed Big Barn, pictured in the upper middle. Bouts featured both local and West Texas fighters. Snipe Conley organized a wartime four-team BLOC softball league. (Mr. and Mrs. Roy Gardner Collection, Petroleum Museum.)

Fishing was also popular. Favored destinations were Spring Creek in nearby Mertzon and Devil's River on the Hudspeth Ranch near Juno. Fishing trips were often multi-family, several-day camping getaways. Men fished, children swam and played, and women cooked and visited. The catches generated a big fish fry, topped off with homemade freezer ice cream, which children eagerly anticipated. Men-only outings occurred at a distant, hard-to-reach spot on the Rio Grande that the at-ease men below successfully visited in 1937. Reclining, left to right, are Bill Spraggins, R.C. Marshall, and Jack Stewart. Sitting, left to right, are Bob Adams and Red Pool. (Both, JSW.)

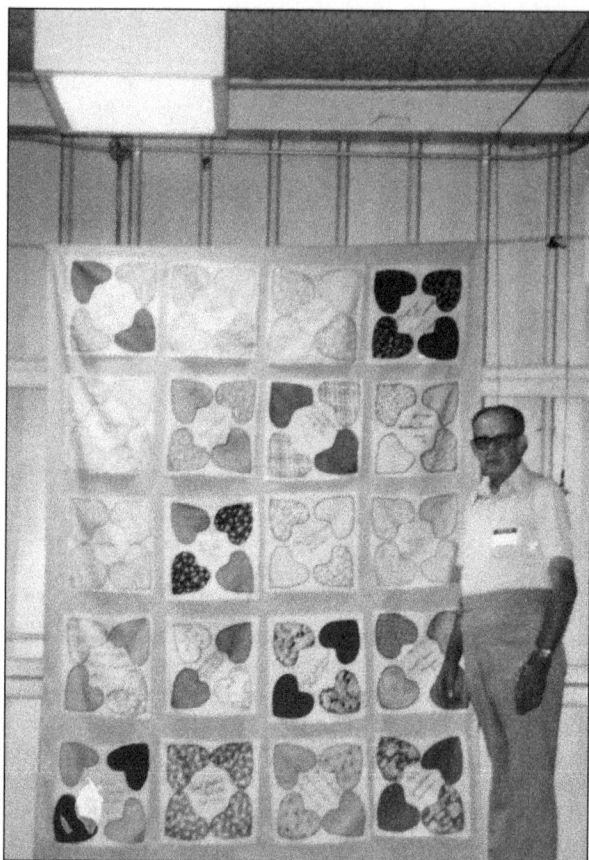

Texon women quilted in each other's homes, according to no set schedule. A quilt frame hung from the ceiling with a pulley that allowed the quilt to be raised and lowered. Quilting went on throughout the day, and the hostess provided the meat for a potluck lunch, which also included working husbands. Quilters' children took their lunches to school and gathered after class to play until their mothers finished. Quilts, made from patterns, scraps, and "strings," were put to home use in the 1930s. In the early 1940s, quilting expanded and served the needy. Quilters included Ada Adams, Olive Cook, Lida Mae Howard, Bessie Reed, Gert Satterfield, Bernice Spraggins, and Pearl Stevens. Pictured at left, Bob Adams, the husband of a quilter, admires a quilt, photographed several years after its completion. Each square bore an appliqué heart and the quilter's embroidered name. (Photograph by James A. Wilson.)

In 1937, a total of 16 charter members founded the Texon Study Club. They elected Corinne Compton president, set dues at $1, limited membership to 18, and published their first program schedule. The program's cover is shown here. They also chose club colors and a motto: "Rest I Rust; Work I Win." Subsequent presidents were Eileen Arledge, Crystal Smith, Doris Way, Fay Grissett, Vivian Ham, and Lilla Beyer. Members read papers and reviewed books relating to yearlong topics, like "Study of Texas" and "The War on the Home Front." The club held an annual tea for nonmembers, sponsored the Texon Library, and, in 1941, with San Angelo's Art Club, hosted an exhibit. In 1945, the Texon Study Club joined the Texas Federation of Women's Clubs. The club, whose last yearbook appeared in 1946, supported the library and remained active through the 1950s. (Crystal Smith.)

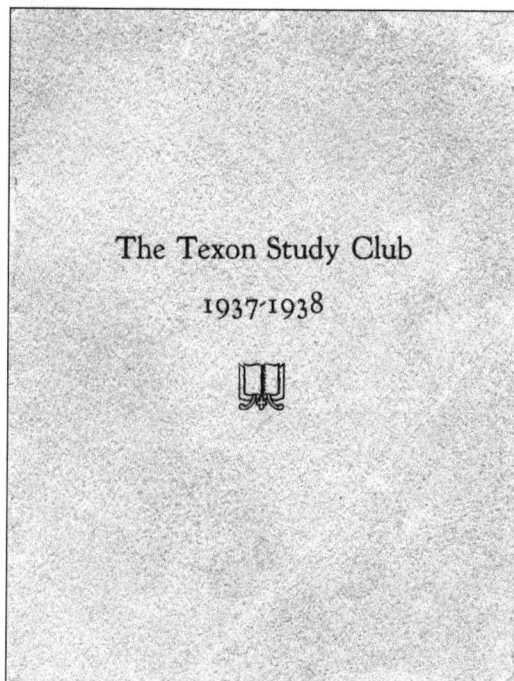

The Texon Study Club

1937-1938

In 1934, both Camp Fire Girls, lead by Helen Elrod and Fay Grissett, and Girl Scouts, under Chlo Harris and Mrs. Neil Stallard, of Santa Rita, were active. By the spring of 1935, only the Girl Scouts were in the news. They gained new "Tenderfeet," spruced up the company-provided meetinghouse, participated in the Poppy Day drive, and attended Camp Louis Farr. In 1936, Harris's troop numbered about 24 members. The summer of 1941 found Girl Scouts—including Maxine Adams, Patsy Ruth Adams, Gisele Goble, Geraldine Rogers, Lois Satterfield, Edna Smelser, Jane Spraggins, and Elaine Sutton—collecting tinfoil for bomb-ravaged England and accepting new members Juanita Harris, Wanda Jackson, and Loraine Poehler. They attended Camp Louis Farr, swam and picnicked on the Pecos River, and chose patrol leaders at an October wiener roast in the Scout House, which the girls sometimes used. (Linda Kaufmann.)

The Cub Scouts were first organized in April 1935, under the auspices of the Texon Union Church. In May 1938, Blondie Menielle was the Cubmaster. Reorganized in August 1942, Cubmaster W.C. LeMeilleur was assisted by B.B. Kelly, and a Cub Parents Association was the sponsor. R.S. Meroney chaired the Pack Committee. Cubs were Bobbie Baker, Donald Criswell, Raymond Garrison, John Glidewell, Raymond Jackson, Jamie Kelly, Johnny McMillan, Bobby Meroney, Pat Shattuck, and Larry Smith. In the spring of 1945, Cubmaster Menielle and Troop 3055 held den meetings and presented awards at Camp Louis Farr. Pictured in the early 1940s is Cub Rex Spraggins. (JSW.)

News Letter No. 24

To Big Lake Oil Company Employees in the Armed Services:

This is the second anniversary of the News Letter. We hope that it has served its purpose in keeping you advised of local happenings and of the whereabouts and activities of your friends in the services. Our aim has been to let you know that you are not alone - that your arduous tasks and heavy burdens are being shared by others, and that the home fires are kept burning, awaiting your return. Perhaps it has served in refreshing your memory of fond recollections or by its levity has dispelled some of the gloom that so frequently besets those away from home. We hope so - and if so, shall feel well-repaid. We also hope that this will be the last anniversary of the News Letter - that next year you will all be at home safe and sound and happy in the knowledge of a dangerous and dirty job well done.

Texon's World War II commitment was total. Patriotic rallies and a student essay contest preceded Pearl Harbor. Appeals from the Red Cross, headed locally by "Mom" Workman, yielded cash donations that exceeded quotas. Teenage girls knitted sweaters for servicemen, and women spent countless hours folding bandages and making pajamas and baby clothes. County war bond chairman Ted Williams and Texon workers like Corinne Compton and Edna Stewart put the 1943 drive "over the top" by $15,000, which included $20,000 from BLOC. Charles Beyer directed a two-county oil field scrap iron effort, provided a plot for the town's Victory Garden, and delayed applying Daylight Savings Time in order to extend the winter workday. From December 15, 1942, through 1945, Beyer sent a monthly newsletter, as pictured, to those in uniform. (LBC.)

In 1941, before Pearl Harbor, Texon men were called up under the draft act of 1940, and many volunteered, such as those pictured at right. They are, from left to right, Cecil Delz, R.W. Spraggins, and Eddie Ringle, all of whom entered the Army Air Corps (AAC). Delz and Spraggins remained stateside. Ringle, a B-24 gunner, was wounded over Germany. His father, A.L. "Babe" Ringle, also of Texon, served 23 months with the Seabees in the South Pacific. Another AAC enlistee, Ray Cook, pictured below, earned his wings and qualified to fly the B-17 Flying Fortress. (Right, R.W. Spraggins; below, JSW.)

Pictured at left is Marion Spraggins. Upon graduation from Reagan County High School, he joined the Navy. As an electrician's mate, he was assigned to a Landing Ship, Tank (LST) and participated in several South Pacific island campaigns. Mike Adams, pictured below, was commissioned in the Navy Air Corps and trained to fly the Helldiver, a carrier-based dive-bomber. (Both, JSW.)

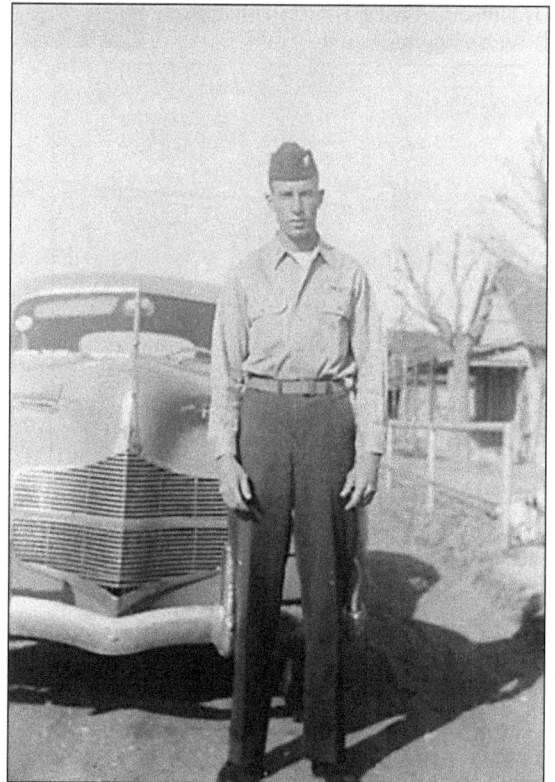

Carl D. "Don" Warriner, inducted in the summer of 1944, served with the 357th Infantry in Germany in the spring of 1945. Pictured at right, he earned the Silver Star for valor in the face of the enemy. He campaigned through Germany into Czechoslovakia and was reassigned to occupation duty in Germany, which included guarding war criminals at Nuremberg. Pictured below is Paul McCollum, who entered the Army Air Corps in the spring of 1943, trained as a bombardier, and was commissioned in October. He was with the Fifteenth Air Force in Italy during the summer of 1944. Awarded the Air Medal, he was reassigned stateside. (Both, LBC.)

Army engineer Gene Warriner, shown at left, was killed during the D-Day invasion when his landing craft struck a mine and sank. Just two weeks earlier, he had married an Englishwoman, Evelyn Carson, who eventually married Gene's brother, Don, and became an American citizen. Wendell Pearce, below, grew up in Texon. An Army pilot, he died when his plane crashed during a solo flight near Ballinger, Texas, in 1942. Two others—Bill Agnew, son of driller W.H. Agnew, and former Oiler Jack Brown—were killed in action on the Western Front in 1944 and 1945, respectively. (Left, Richard Warriner; below, JSW.)

Because the National Guard had been federalized, the Texas Legislature, in response to President Roosevelt's appeal, created the Texas Defense Guard in 1941, which was also called the Home Guard. It was formed to deter sabotage and render disaster assistance. Reagan County's quota for Company C included 75 members. Sheriff A.W. Billingsley was its first captain, and Texon's Bob Harvey and C.C. Sandy were lieutenants. BLOC loaned $500 to buy uniforms, and the guard was issued rifles for target practice and drill. In January 1942, the public was invited to view maneuvers in Texon. In January 1943, officers attended a weeklong training session in San Antonio, and in September, the unit participated in weekend maneuvers in Abilene. Company C also marched in parades. Approximately 25 Texon men, most of them pictured, were Guard members. (Clayton Bird.)

The January 1944 marriage of Charles Beyer and former Texon teacher Lilla Hickerson brought graciousness and warmth to the general manager's residence. Pictured below, it became the setting for dinner and card parties and was, in essence, a hotel for important visitors. His wife's cheerful, outgoing qualities offset Beyer's self-admitted social reticence. Because of her earlier stay in Texon (1930–1936), she felt she "had come back home." She had always liked Texon and became actively involved in its life, because, she said, "We get out of a community what we put into it." Lilla was a definite asset for "Charlie" during their 31-year marriage. (Both, LBC.)

African Americans, though little-noted, were present. They worked in service capacities, such as garbage collectors, hospital porters, café cooks, and domestics. Levi Smith employed a black couple, William and Annie Baismore, as a butler and cook and provided a retirement fund for them. Pictured at right is William Baismore. Below is Corinne Freeman, a housekeeper for Lilla Beyer, who praised her character and work ethic. Beyer also thought highly of Grace Thompson and Earl Allen, whom Charles Beyer had previously retained. West Texas held little appeal for African Americans because so few lived there. (Right, Jane Ransom Lynch; below, LBC.)

On Victory over Japan Day, August 15, 1945, church bells rang in Texon—and throughout America—and residents gathered at the picnic grounds, pictured above, to celebrate. At the serving table below are, from left to right, Hattie Bird, unidentified, Lena Stewart, and unidentified. At least 105 individuals from Texon, or roughly 13 percent of the 1940 population (800), entered the armed services. They served in the North African, European, and Pacific theaters of action, to a much lesser extent in Asia, and a considerable number were stationed at American installations. Interestingly, Johnny Mack Garrison was part of screen actress Joan Blondell's USO troupe of entertainers. Clearly significant was the Big Lake Field's contribution, which, from 1941 through 1945, amounted to approximately 1.3 percent of the nation's oil output. (Both, Hattie Bird.)

Three

THE LATER YEARS

The disappointing wartime drilling results meant that until 1962, the Big Lake Field's operations were largely "routine," as one BLOC office worker observed in early 1946. Five years later, it was judged to be a "pumping field," and drilling had become unimportant. During the 1950s, output decreased between three and four percent annually. In 1952, when an explosion destroyed the gasoline plant, an unpromising future ruled out rebuilding, and four years later, Plymouth took over BLOC and shifted management responsibilities to its Midland office. All the while, the production and profit slide continued. In 1961, for the first time in the company's history, Plymouth's directors could not declare a stock dividend and decided to liquidate. The following year, Plymouth sold out to Ohio Oil, soon to become Marathon Oil, for approximately $58 million—and Texon as a company town was no more.

No matter what, decline was an all-too-apparent theme, but those who remained in Texon kept the community spirit alive. Though retirements and transfers shrunk their numbers, residents did not stint in their support of the town's young people and their recreational and school-related activities. They remained dedicated to the Texon Union Church and its Sunday school classes, revivals, and vacation Bible school programs. They helped each other, like disabled Mack Irby, and those in need, such as Ozona's flood victims.

Were they disheartened as the Texon School's enrollment dwindled, businesses closed, and Plymouth no longer funded the Labor Day celebration and the company Christmas party? Undoubtedly. But Texon residents were also proud, especially when in October 1959, forty-one current Plymouth employees and retirees were honored as Permian Basin Petroleum Pioneers. For three decades and more, they and their families were loyal to BLOC-Plymouth and the town it created, and because of their loyalty, the Texon story continues to be told.

And while "the old home town" of poet Angie Fell Hasty might have been "laid to rest," its descendants gather each year, "their memories . . . drawn to . . . Texon."

In May 1950, after 18 years as BLOC vice president and general manager, Charles E. Beyer retired and is pictured at the desk employees presented to him. He continued Levi Smith's policies and advised those with problems. Alert to "loansharking," in March 1942, Beyer suggested formation of the employee-owned Texon Federal Credit Union, which, by early 1948, had loaned more than $27,000. He wrote a wartime newsletter, guaranteed veterans company jobs, and counseled young men to seek careers beyond a futureless Texon. He was critical to building the Scout House, allowed the Girl Scouts and Brownies use of a company house, authorized upkeep of the golf course and other facilities, and sustained the money-losing postwar theater. Perhaps not "one of the boys," his commitment to Texon, nevertheless, was genuine. He died in 1975, and his widow, Lilla, died in 2003. (Photograph by BT.)

Charles Beyer's retirement meant that W.J. "Whitey" Grissett became general manager. Prior to his appointment, he had risen from pipeliner to gang pusher, to assistant superintendent, and to superintendent. He is pictured with his wife, Fay, and sons Charles, left, and John David. A civic-minded company man, he served as Cubmaster for several years, was active in the church and Sunday school, oversaw development of the new picnic grounds in 1952, and provided materials for the church nursery. In 1956, when Plymouth absorbed BLOC, Grissett was transferred to Plymouth's Midland office. (JSW.)

In 1950, when Whitey Grissett became BLOC's general manager, Clint Satterfield, one of many West Virginians who arrived in Texon in 1924, became general superintendent. He and his wife, Gert, pictured at right, were parents of two daughters, Corrine and Lois, and a son, Monroe. In 1956, Grissett's transfer to Midland elevated Satterfield to general manager and another West Virginian, Cliff Newbrough, to superintendent. Newbrough came to Texon in 1924 as a driller and was hired on with BLOC in 1925. At Satterfield's death in 1958, Elson Shattuck, who joined BLOC in 1928, took his place. Shattuck is pictured below with his wife, Mae. They had three boys, Gene, Lloyd, and Pat, and two girls, Betty and Margie. (Both, JSW.)

Coming out of the war, the previously all-male office staff revealed a feminine look that would remain. To Charles Beyer, it seemed that men and women "get along . . . nicely and there is a more genteel atmosphere." The following office workers from the early 1950s are, from left to right: (first row) Osa Goble, Jo Sandy, Frank Shepard, Cliff Newbrough, and Golda Edwards; (second row) Jim Isbell, Leonard Lee, general manager Whitey Grissett, Lloyd Killam, Clint Satterfield, and Earl Brooks. Golda Edwards, assistant to chief clerk Jim Isbell, stayed the longest of the women employees. Personnel reductions occurred throughout the 1950s, especially in 1956, when Plymouth absorbed BLOC. (Fay Grissett.)

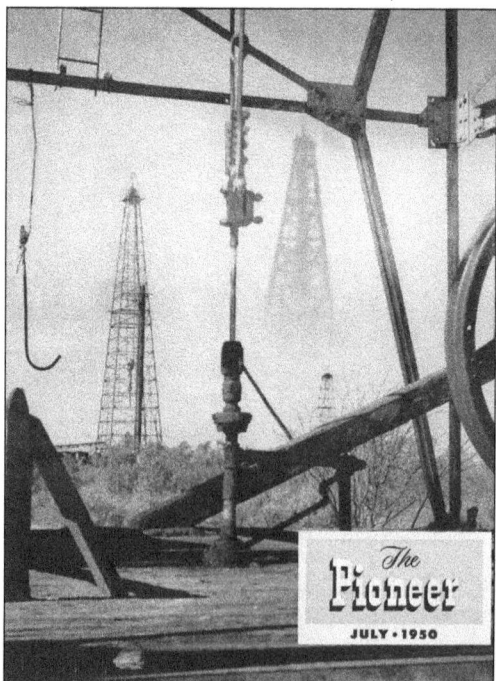

The Loose Leaf, B-T's monthly magazine, published from 1946 to 1950. Its successor, the Pioneer, ran from 1950 through 1961. On its July 1950 cover is an old-time wooden BLOC derrick floor with a modern drilling rig. Both publications carried a much-anticipated, people-oriented "Texon Tidings" section that was the responsibility of BLOC office worker Jack Hitt (1946–August 1950); Mack Irby, Texon postmaster (September 1950–December 1952); Fay Grissett, wife of general manager Whitey Grissett (June 1953–January 1956); Ione Isbell, wife of office employee Jim Isbell (February–September 1956); and various others in later years. Bill Thompson, who transferred from Texon to Plymouth's Sinton office, was a photographer for both magazines. (Magazine courtesy BT.)

In the late 1940s and 1950s, drilling was modest at best. In 1950–1951, BLOC partnered with Stanolind Oil and Gas on a 40-acre tract slightly southwest of Texon and brought in a discovery well that spurred activity in the deep Fusselman pay level. As Santa Rita No. 1 plugged along at about six barrels a day, University of Texas's royalties from the Big Lake Field through 1950 totaled more than $110 million. In 1953, located in section 11 and just north of Texon, University No. 1-11 (pictured at right) came in at the Ellenberger level and sparked talk of a new deep pool. Hopes were dashed, however, as the field's output fell sharply through 1961. BLOC hands being transported to the field are pictured below. (Both, JDG, Petroleum Museum.)

In late 1947, Plymouth Oil and Slick-Urschel brought in the discovery well of the Sarah Benedum Field in neighboring Upton County. Named for Mike Benedum's wife, its promise of becoming a major field justified construction of a camp, the temporary sign for which is pictured above, with dormitories and houses, and it drew experienced BLOC hands. Texon residents who moved or commuted to Benedum Field included those pictured below. They are, from left to right, Bill Mac Varnadore, Orvel Gryder, Jim Newbrough, L.B. "Blondie" Menielle, and Jack Stewart. Two more were Clarence Hickle, the Texon gas plant superintendent who supervised construction of plants at Sinton and Benedum, and J.D. Norwood, a BLOC employee since 1929 and the power plant's chief engineer. Other Plymouth holdings, like the Susan Peak Field in Tom Green County and Crockett County's Olson Field, also depleted Texon's population. (Photographs by BT.)

On October 20, 1951, at the Petroleum Club in Midland, Plymouth Oil honored 41 men employed 25 years or more. All had started with Plymouth-BLOC in Texon. They received diamond-studded watches from Plymouth president Walter S. Hallanan, pictured second row, second from right. In the first row, far right, is L.M. "Boob" Davis, hired in January 1924—BLOC's first Texas employee. The following men, from left to right, are other 1924 Texon pioneers: (first row) Curtis Howard, fourth from left, and Davis; (second row) H.H. Talley, far left, and J.J. Isbell, far right; (fifth row) Clint Satterfield, far right; (sixth row) Bob Adams, Whitey Grissett, Mike Griffith, and L.B. Menielle, sixth from left. Others not pictured are A.A. Criswell, Cliff Newbrough, and Jess Newbrough. (JSW.)

Plymouth's 1951 awards ceremony included wives of the honorees. In West Texas, they faced an often-harsh environment, isolation, and long distances from loved ones. Yet they persisted, raised families, and helped create a caring, accepting community. Those who came in 1924 with their husbands are (first row) Ada Adams, third from right; (second row) Gert Satterfield, third from right; and (fourth row) Viola Talley, sixth from right. Teachers who married after arriving are (third row) Norine Menielle, far left, and Marie McCollum, third from left. Ione Isbell, third row, second from left, came as a nurse and then married. BLOC office worker Golda Rogers, second row, second from left, married in Texon. (JSW.)

Leonard Scott purchased the Texon Grocery Store in 1946. He expanded into the adjoining Texon Library's room; added frozen food, variety, and dry goods sections; and installed a produce cooler. Early 1950s employees included longtime resident Gert Satterfield and Leonard's brother Clyde. Inducted during the Korean War, Scott sold his inventory to his father-in-law, C.C. Higday, of Rankin. In July 1954, Tom Reed, of San Angelo, became manager. He stayed until early 1955, when Clyde Scott took over and remained until August 1959. When the store closed in 1960, so did a community asset. It had hosted bake sales, assisted in selling Girl Scout cookies, and contributed to the purchase of local boy Johnny Gibbs's prize lamb. The store's exterior, pictured in earlier years, remained unchanged. (Paul Burton Collection, Petroleum Museum.)

In 1948, Mae and Elson Shattuck, owners of the refurbished Texon Café, profited from the opening of nearby Benedum Field. W.H. Moore succeeded the Shattucks, and in 1950, "Mom" and "Dad" Wright, the original owners, again took over. Dad and teacher Marie Rhodes McCollum are pictured above. Teacher Rosamond Rentz is below at the café's side door. Subsequent owners were Ben and Veda Bowen, Bill Humphrey, Frank and Irma Jacot, and, on two occasions, Dale and Flo Gardner. The Texon Café hosted coffees, golf tournament dinners, birthday celebrations, and World Series watchers. Its employees included Jonnie Keight, Margaret Gooch, Pearlie Mae Garrett, and Ida Kerlin, who worked for five owners. Dorothy Gardner Davis remembers her parents' waitresses in white uniforms. In 1960, the county's oldest café closed with its reputation for quality intact. (Both, Maxine Adams Hyden.)

In 1948, Red Rogers sold the Texon Drugstore to former owner H.S. "Doc" Monroe. In June, BLOC rig builders renovated the store, and Monroe installed lower-wattage fluorescent lighting. Monroe hired Texon teenagers and women, including Maxine Adams and Roxie Garrison. The drugstore's fountain and nickelodeon attracted both adults and the younger set. It was the oil field bus line stop and the pick-up and drop-off place for company field workers, as pictured. In 1960, the Texas Board of Pharmacy honored Monroe for his 50 years in the profession. The drugstore was the last business to close. (JDG, Petroleum Museum.)

In 1943, Betty (Wilkinson) Irby, formerly of Santa Rita, took over the post office when her husband, W.M. "Mack" Irby, who was postmaster since 1942, contracted rheumatoid arthritis. Pres. Harry Truman approved her lifetime appointment in 1946. Postwar postal clerks were Delbert Glenn, Harriet Calhoon, Nell Sullivan, Bertha Delz, and Flo Gardner. In 1958, Betty delivered the Texon pouch to the Overland Mail Centennial Caravan, which retraced the Butterfield Overland Mail route. In 1962, she moved to the Fort Worth Post Office. Pictured in the 1990s are Jane Spraggins Wilson and her brother R.W. Spraggins outside the "new" post office, which was relocated from the Texon Drug Building to San Jacinto Street in 1962. (Photograph by James A. Wilson.)

Stricken with rheumatoid arthritis, Mack Irby, postmaster from 1942 to 1946, received an outpouring of love. In return, he exemplified courage, dignity, and hope. Unable to walk, he was never idle. He sold imported water, prepared tax returns, became a ham radio operator, and wrote for the *Pioneer*. Friends gave him a television set and high-tech wheelchairs and built access ramps. They rigged an exercise apparatus over his bed and a lift for his water exercise tank. And the Texon Hospital never billed him. After he and his wife, Betty (pictured), moved to Fort Worth, he died from surgical complications in April 1962. The many who attended his Big Lake burial could take comfort in his written words, "I'm the luckiest guy in the world. I live in Texon . . . among . . . the finest people in the world." (LBC.)

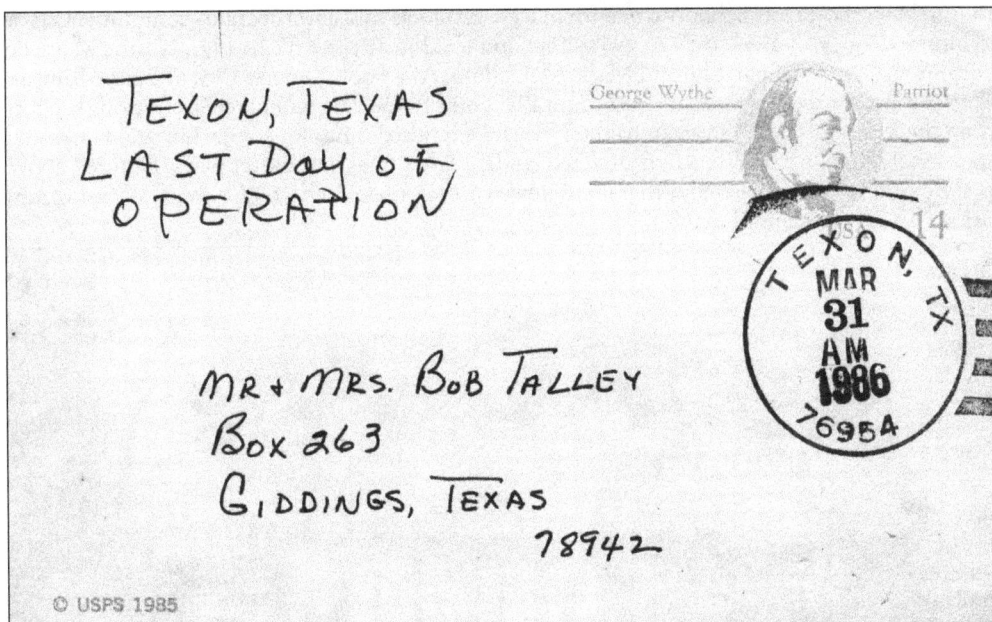

When the Irbys left, Bertha McLeod Delz, postal clerk since 1953, became the acting postmaster until Pres. John F. Kennedy appointed her permanently in 1963. In Texon since 1937, she completed a beautician's course and worked in the beauty shop until her 1940 marriage to Frankie Delz. As postmaster, she and the post office served Marathon Oil employees and area ranchers. She stayed on until the post office closed on March 31, 1986, as indicated by this postmarked card. (Bob Talley.)

In July 1946, the Texon School's three-room west wing was sold amid declining enrollments that fell from 95 in 1943–1944 to 79 in 1945–1946 and to 32 in 1950–1951. In 1947, Norine Menielle became the last principal. She and Marie McCollum, Alla Pool, Nanette Day, and Elsie Runyan were the longest-serving teachers in the late 1940s and 1950s. The school received strong support from the Mothers' Club, successor to the PTA, which raised funds for equipment and books and sponsored school parties. Teachers directed student Christmas and Easter plays. Pictured above is the cast of a 1951 Christmas program. Below is a 1953 student choir. (Above, R.W. Spraggins; below, JDG, Petroleum Museum.)

During 1953–1954, the Texon School's third- and fourth-graders studied the habits of wild birds, built birdhouses, and joined the Junior Audubon Club, whose monthly publication had carried their pictures. Seen above are, from left to right, (first row) Daniel Whitworth, Johnny Ratliff, Jimmy Parker, Larry Gryder, and James Earl Potter; (second row) Drenda Glenn, Virginia Parker, Gay Scott, Kay Armstrong, Jerry Ellen Emerson, Kay Varnadore, Mary Ann Armstrong, and Carolyn Howard. The teacher is Elsie Runyan. She also organized and directed students in a recorder (English flute) band. (Fay Grissett.)

Pictured are the last fifth- and sixth-graders to attend the Texon School. Beginning in 1954–1955, students in those grades were bused to Big Lake. Those pictured are, from left to right, (first row) Donnie Gryder, Allen Wilson, Mack Siegenthaler, Ronnie Gryder, and Don Stacy; (second row) LaJean Scott, Francine Salyer, Barbara Moore, Linda Way, Kate Armstrong, and Sandra Tessier; (third row) Gigette Goertz, Pat Miller, and Jo Whitehead. The teacher is Nanette Day. Patricia Whitworth was absent on the day of the photograph. For 1956–1957, the third and fourth grades were moved to Big Lake. Norine Menielle, who first joined the faculty in 1929, taught first and second grades and was the only teacher during the 1956–1957 and 1957–1958 school years. Texon School closed in 1958. (Fay Grissett.)

Texon students were achievers at Reagan County High School. Edna Smelser (1946), Betty Louise Howard (1950), and Charles Grissett (1955) were valedictorians of their classes, and Bill Slatton (1951), Dorothy Owens (1953), and James Whitehead (1958) were salutatorians of their classes. Texon graduates with averages above 90 in 1953 were Ann Way, Bobbie Malone, and Jerry Thompson. Bob Adams, longtime BLOC employee, served several terms on the school board and was president in 1955. The RCHS band had a strong Texon presence and received support from an active Texon–Big Lake Band Parents Club. Texon members consistently finished high in University Interscholastic League competitions. Band majorettes from Texon (T) and Big Lake (BL) pictured in 1949 are, from left to right, (first row) Tibba McMillan (BL); (second row) Dixie McMillan (BL), twins Helen and Mildred Norwood (T), and Lois Ann Spraggins (T), the chosen drum majorette in 1950. (Photograph by Ed Phy, courtesy Debi Scott.)

After the war, the Texon Union Church remained vital. The lack of a full-time minister meant reliance upon area clergy, most of them from Big Lake, Crane, and Rankin. They were primarily from Baptist and Disciples of Christ churches; others were from Methodist, Presbyterian, and Church of Christ denominations. Texon-born Bob Talley preached occasionally to capacity congregations. Typically, Sunday services were held in the afternoon, with Sunday school in the morning. After the theater burned, the church hosted the company Christmas party, and the choir performed for those in attendance in 1950. Choir members are, from left to right, Bob Adams, Leonard Scott, Gert Satterfield, Pat Adams, Pearl Oldham, Sondra Thompson, Diana Lee Salyer, and Leonard Lee. (Fay Grissett.)

The church and its active Sunday school supported the annual vacation Bible school, a Bible study program, and a series of revivals conducted by laymen, divinity students, and ordained ministers. Several young Texon men, including Leonard Bird, Leonard Lee, Eddie McMillan, Lloyd Shattuck, Charles Shook, and Bob Talley, pursued ministerial studies in the early 1950s and returned to preach. BLOC provided materials for members to add a nursery, and the Texon School's recorder band, directed by Elsie Runyan and pictured in 1953, contributed to Sunday services. (JDG, Petroleum Museum.)

In 1948, the Texon Vacation Bible School, sponsored by the Sunday school, enrolled 53 children. In 1950, Baylor University students directed the program. In 1951, Big Lake's First Baptist Church was the sponsor, and in 1952, the Methodist Church of Big Lake assisted. In 1954 and 1955, 103 and 85 children participated. The Sunday school—which was comprised of the women's Fidelis and LWT classes, the men's class, and the young people's and primary classes—also held holiday parties and picnics, contributed to needy families, and sponsored outings. Leonard Lee, Sunday school superintendent for seven years, retired in 1953 and is pictured with his wife, Elizabeth (Smelser), longtime primary class teacher, and son Barton. Lee left to study for the ministry. (LBC.)

Although the Texon Hospital had no full-time doctor in 1945–1946, nurses like Texon-born Dorothy (Criswell) Sawyer and longtime resident Cordie Lee (Harris) Ledbetter were on the job. Dr. J.L. Wright arrived in December 1946, and he and several long-serving nurses, including Ned Malone and cousins Jean and Patsy Safley, treated a great number of oil field injuries, the result of increased postwar drilling. O.W. Harris replaced Wright in 1948 and left in early 1949, when Phil Dandrea came and stayed until the hospital closed in August 1950. Veteran employees Mrs. O.D. Lovell, dietician, and James Freeman, porter, also worked until the end. Nurses Margaret Palmer and Ione Isbell staffed a first aid station until 1962. The hospital building (pictured) was sold, moved to Big Lake, and converted into apartments. (JDG, Petroleum Museum.)

By 1945, the era of extras, like bank nights and talent shows, was over at the Texon Theatre, pictured above. Johnny and Era Flynn continued as managers, and even though a shrinking population and competition from Big Lake's new drive-in caused it to operate at a loss, BLOC kept the theater open for its employees. On June 10, 1950, an early morning blaze destroyed the building, despite the efforts of firefighters from two towns and the use of a well service pumper truck. The last film shown was *The Rustlers*, an RKO "shoot 'em up." Another loss occurred when the Big Barn collapsed, pictured below, during a strong wind in 1954. Used to store company vehicles, it had also served as a gymnasium. (Above, Ann Way Schneemann; below, JDG, Petroleum Museum.)

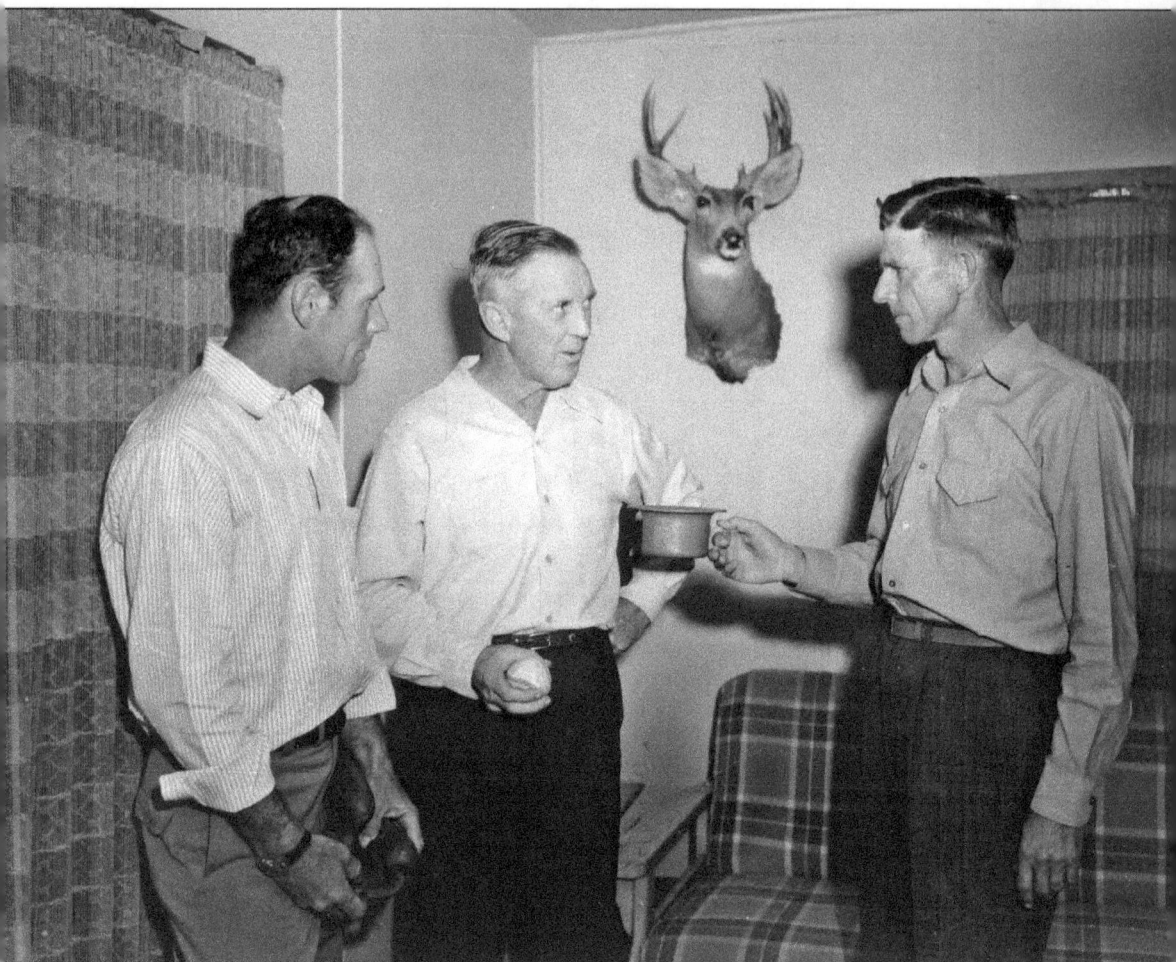

The Oilers would never say die. In 1949, Snipe Conley managed a Big Lake–Texon team with several ex-Oilers in the Permian Basin League—and won the title. From that club, pitcher Bud Jordan signed with the National League's Boston Braves. The team also included brothers Marvin "Big Gussy" and Cliff "Little Gussy" Gustafson, who played two seasons. Cliff eventually became the winningest baseball coach (until 2005) in NCAA Division I history at the University of Texas, Austin. From 1950 to 1953, the Big Lake Snipers, including former Oilers, played in the Concho Basin League. In 1953, old Oilers pitcher Archie Peel was manager. In 1955, Conley was one of the *Houston Chronicle*'s "Sports Heroes of Yesteryear." Two years later, his retirement officially ended the Oilers chapter. He is pictured between ex-Oiler Frank "Lefty" Jacot, left, and Raymond Thompson. (Photograph by BT.)

Youth baseball flourished briefly. In 1946, "Lefty" Jacot and Archie Peel coached the Reagan County High School team. In 1950, Curtis Barbee guided the church-sponsored Little Oilers. Players included Clay Barbee, Dale Calley, Roy Fell, Charles Grissett, Roger Goertz, Oliver Wendell Parker, Jerry Thompson, and Ralph Way. Barbee coached the team in 1951 and 1952. In 1953, he and Snipe Conley were coach and manager of a Texon–Big Lake Little League team, and Barbee also coached a two-town teenage team. Pictured above, in 1953, are Barbee, left, and Conley. Below is 1953 Little League team member Riley Spraggins. In 1954, Barbee and ex-Oiler George Dykes coached a Big Lake–sponsored teenage team that included Texon boys Clay Barbee, Joe Lee Kosel, Marvin Morris, and Mack Siegenthaler. (Both, JSW.)

Labor Day Barbecue - Big Lake Oil Co., Texon, Texas. 1948

Postwar Labor Day celebrations, though smaller than before, were well-attended. They included a ceremony introduced in 1944 by Charles Beyer that awarded 5-, 10-, 15-, 20-, and 25-year pins and gifts and the recognition of retirees. Retiree Ervin Cagle is pictured above facing Beyer in 1948. The celebrations once again featured R.J. Cook's barbecued beef, and in 1948, the 500 who gathered were served 735 pounds of meat, 100 pounds of pinto beans, and 140 pounds of potato salad. Despite threatening weather, some 450 attended in 1950 and saw a rain-shortened game between Oilers old-timers and the Big Lake club. The 1952 event inaugurated the new picnic grounds at the base of Golf Hill, whose covered serving area is pictured below. (Above, Ettawah Cagle Morris; below, JDG, Petroleum Museum.)

At the 1953 Labor Day celebration, Bob Adams and his fellow BLOC employees were, as they had been for years, on hand to prepare beans and potato salad, fill plates, and clean up. Adams is pictured above in the center of his 1953 crew. In 1955, the Odessa Chuck Wagon Gang, pictured below, prepared and served barbecue and trimmings. (Both, Fay Grissett.)

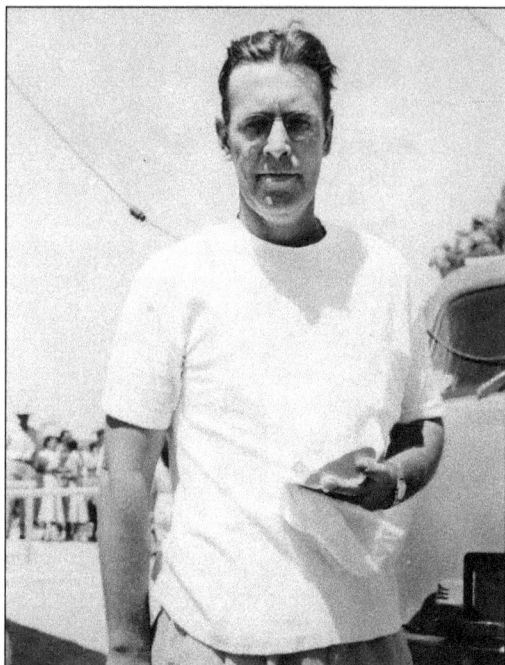

About 650 attended the 1954 Labor Day celebration and witnessed the presentation of service awards to 12 men. Two of those recognized were Bill Miller, pictured at left, a 15-year BLOC employee, and Earl Holmes, a five-year man. Holmes is pictured below to the right of retiree Jim Jones. (Left, Fay Grissett; below, JDG, Petroleum Museum.)

The 1955 Labor Day celebration was the last. Mike Griffith, who started with BLOC in 1924 and rose to become Plymouth's general manager, died in 1954. He had supported the Labor Day tradition. His successor, Gordon Fisher, did not. This annual event, wrote Fay Grissett, was "looked forward to with great anticipation," and especially so in later years when the growing number of retirees who had left looked forward to returning for a day of fellowship. Pearl Oldham, wife of a longtime employee, called it "akin to a family reunion." In 1956, some who had not been notified arrived, and in a typical Texon gesture, residents eased their disappointment by bringing food to the picnic grounds. Pictured in 1955 are those who were employed 25 years or longer. (Fay Grissett.)

The 3,078-yard Colina Alta course was a hotbed of activity. Every year in the late 1940s and 1950s, the club hosted an invitational tournament, which drew some 110 entrants in 1952. Texon's Oliver "Boob" Howard was a five-time winner of the event, for which merchants donated prizes. BLOC provided sand and oil for the "greens," and club members supplied the maintenance. Avid golfers included Trigg Housewright, Frank Jacot, Billy Keene, Eddie McMillan Jr., O.W. Parker, Leonard Scott, Gene and Lloyd Shattuck, Bill Mack Varnadore, Troy White, and W.T. Wilson. In 1951, Texon entered a team in the Permian Basin Golf League, and several players did well in area tournaments. Talented junior golfers were Clay Barbee and James Whitehead. Pictured on the tee box is Vonnie Brown. (Vonnie Brown.)

Holes	Yards	Par						Holes	Yards	Par				
1	354	4						1	354	4				
2	164	3						2	164	3				
3	415	4						3	415	4				
4	494	5						4	494	5				
5	354	4						5	354	4				
6	552	5						6	552	5				
7	128	3						7	128	3				
8	296	4						8	296	4				
9	321	4						9	321	4				
Out	3078	36						In	3078	36				
COLINA ALTA GOLF CLUB								Out	3078	36				
								Tot.	6156	72				

Women also took up golf. They sponsored at least five club tournaments during the 1950s. Florence Gardner, Dorothy Howard, Irma Jacot, Marian (Gray) Wilson, and Maxine (Adams) Wimberley were among the active players. Irma Jacot dominated Colina Alta tournaments and frequently won or placed in area events. At Fort Stockton in 1952, Dorothy Howard faced a new hazard: grass. "I couldn't do a thing" on that "frog hair," she commiserated, until she realized "it was just pure dee old grass." Couples golf also proved popular in Texon. Pictured is a Colina Alta scorecard. (Jesse Thompson.)

For Texon youth, the swimming pool, pictured above, was a magnet during the long, hot summers. The diving board and newly installed slide, pictured below, meant fun for both younger children and teenagers. The pool and its clubhouse also provided a setting for parties and picnics. Lifeguards were high school boys like Charles Grissett in 1954 and James Whitehead in 1957. (Above, Maxine Adams Hyden; below, Fay Grissett.)

The tennis courts were well used. BLOC refurbished them in 1948, and the courts were the hosts of a round of tournaments. Female players were active, as were Texon members of Reagan County High School tennis teams and these teenage girls shown in the 1940s. They are, from left to right, (kneeling) Ada Lee Gregg, Jane Spraggins, and Mary Frances Sutton; (standing) Cordie Lee Harris, Helen Stephens, Mary Proctor, Dorothy Criswell, and Marian (Gray) Wilson. Women's softball was also popular, and the Texon Oilerettes, organized in 1950, played area teams. Players were Pat Adams, June Barbee, Irma Jacot, Bobbie Malone, Dorothy Owens, Jean and Patsy Safley, Diana Lee Salyer, Ann Shattuck, Ann Shook, Pat Strain, and Sondra Thompson. Marvin and Cliff Gustafson, members of Snipe Conley's Concho Basin League team, were the manager and water boy, respectively. (JSW.)

The clubhouse continued to vibrate with activity. Its social gatherings included bridal and baby showers, wedding receptions, anniversary celebrations, and coffees and teas. Among those who provided music on such occasions were Pat Adams, Jo Cook, Alice Goble, Luther Louise and Winnie Paul Ham, Dorothy Owens, Oliver Wendell Parker III, and Carla Jo Ratliff. Entertaining became easier when, in 1954, BLOC enclosed the screened porch, which became a much-appreciated kitchen. The Home Demonstration Club raised funds for a new stove, donated shades and curtains, waxed the floors, and painted. As pictured, the porch is to the right of the clubhouse chimney. (Randy King.)

Clubhouse happenings varied. There were holiday, birthday, retirement, and farewell parties. Teenage dances and high school class parties were well-attended, and the Texon Youth Center, formed in 1951, was responsible for raising funds for a new cold drink box and jukebox. There were also 42 (a dominoes game) and bridge parties, as well as the popular Stanley Home Products demonstration parties. At a "tacky" party, in November 1950, Jack Shepard (pictured) and Corrine (Satterfield) Newbrough were judged the "tackiest" man and woman. (JSW.)

Scouting continued to be a major youth activity. At least the following eight boys became Eagle Scouts: in 1946, Bud and J.C. Jordan, Jamie Kelly, Gene and Pat Shattuck, and Harrie Smith; in 1949, Jackie Stewart; and in 1951, polio victim Danny Newbrough. Newbrough received the Eagle Scout badge while he was seated in his wheelchair during rehabilitation. Troop 55 consistently performed well in first aid meets, or "first-aid-o-rees." There were frequent outings to Camp Louis Farr and to the new Camp Sol Meyer, near Fort McKavett. In 1950, three boys (pictured) attended the national jamboree. They are, from left to right, Charles Grissett, Danny Newbrough, and Oliver Wendell Parker III. Scouts collected clothes for Ozona flood victims, undertook a tree-planting project, and maintained invalid Mack Irby's yard. (LBC.)

Dedicated adults sustained Scouting. Scoutmasters for Troop 55 were Leonard Lee (1943–1953), Leon Kessler (1953–1954), Gene Cook (1954–1955, 1956–1957), Don Warriner (1955–1956), Raymond Pierson (1957–1958), and James H. Bird (1958–1961). Cook was also advisor to the Explorers for older youth. Scouters, who were Scout fathers and other supporters like Raymond Thompson, conducted annual finance drives. Many of these Scouters were district officers. They also directed boys in laying water pipes at Camp Louis Farr, Camp Sol Meyer, and at the West Texas Boys' Ranch. Pictured with his wife, Ada, is Bob Adams, a pillar of Texon Scouting. In 1949, he received the Silver Beaver, the highest nonprofessional Scouter award. In 1954, Whitey Grissett was presented the Scouter's Key, the highest unit leader award. Grissett, a longtime Cubmaster, was largely responsible for the Cub Scout program until his transfer in 1956. (Maxine Adams Hyden.)

In late 1953, Girl Scout and Brownie troops were organized. BLOC allowed them to meet in the "Doll House," the former residence of Freck and Fern Siefert. Maxine Wimberley and Iris Salyer lead the Scouts in the 1950s, while Jo Cook, Dorothy Davis, Ethel Ensley, Dorothy Howard, and Janeria (Thomas) Kessler guided the Brownies. Girl Scout Troop 1 gathered clothes for Ozona flood victims, sold cookies, and regularly improved and cleaned the Girl Scout House and its yard. In 1956, they traveled to Carlsbad Caverns, and in 1956, both Scouts and Brownies honored their fathers at a spaghetti dinner. Brownies visited McCamey's radio station and, in 1955, enjoyed an outing in San Antonio. Pictured above in 1954 are members of Troop 1, and pictured at right are their leaders. From left to right are Lola Scott, Maxine Wimberley, and Janeria Kessler. (Both, Maxine Adams Hyden.)

During the Korean War (1950–1953), some two dozen Texon men either enlisted or were inducted. Six served in Korea. In August 1950, Burke Isbell, pictured at left, was the first to be inducted. Orin "Corky" Fell, pictured below, joined the Marines in the fall of 1950. In 1952, Texon-raised George W. Bird, a career naval officer, received commendation for gallantry. Army corporal Rufus Elbert Douglas, nephew of Ben and Artie Howard of Texon, was among 21 prisoners of war who rejected repatriation. A graduate of the Texon School and RCHS, he had been in Boy Scouts and the Home Guard and had enlisted during World War II. Although wounded, he returned to combat prior to capture. He died and is buried in China. (Left, Burke Isbell; below, JDG, Petroleum Museum.)

The Texon Gun Club hosted trap shooting during early Labor Day celebrations. It reappeared in 1960 with a membership of 28. Members practiced at the firing range near the picnic grounds, and many did well in area events. In 1960, L.B. Davis won trophies at McCamey, and in May 1961, J.S. "Shack" Jones took first place at San Angelo. Pictured above are, from left to right, Texon shooters Lacy Way, Joe Kosel, Frankie Delz, Dale Gardner, and Don Warriner. Raymond Thompson is pictured below loading traps. (Photographs by BT.)

The Gun Club sponsored at least two "shoots." The one held in August 1960—a "Ham Shoot"— warranted a two-page piece in the *Pioneer*. Pictured at left is ham winner Gene Cook, who was a Texon-born 43-year employee of BLOC, Plymouth, and Marathon. Below with his prize is Jack Shepard, another Texon native and longtime employee. The club also hosted a shoot in March 1961. (Photographs by BT.)

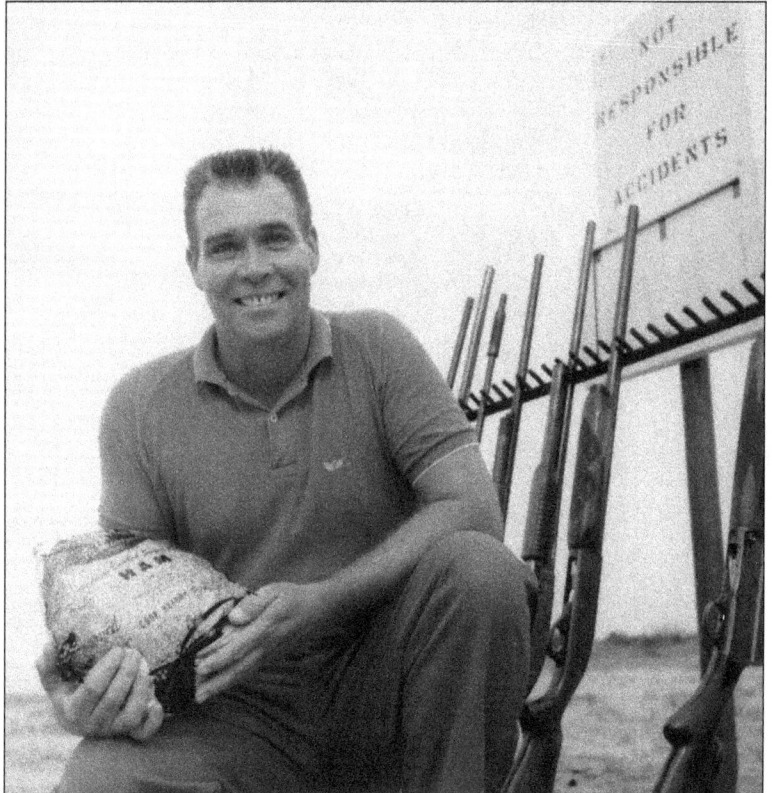

Directed by the Texas Agricultural Extension Service, Home Demonstration Clubs were dedicated to improving home living and supporting girls in 4-H. From 1946 through 1959, the Texon Home Demonstration Club, with women from Santa Rita, Best, and outlying oil camps, worked through county Home Demonstration agents, who offered such programs as furniture refinishing, home finance, and healthful cooking. Members regularly took homemade sweets and reading material to the veterans' and state hospitals in Big Spring and to the West Texas Boys Ranch in nearby Tankersley. Presidents included Vivian Ham, Ethel Ensley, Alice Goble, Pauline Diez, Rose Hughes, and Jo Cook. The club provided an opportunity to learn and socialize for a great many Texon women. Pictured is the cover of the 1958 Home Demonstration yearbook for Reagan County. (Alice Goble.)

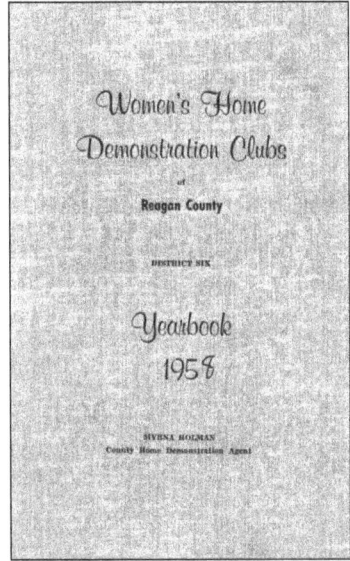

Women's Home
Demonstration Clubs
of
Reagan County

DISTRICT SIX

Yearbook
1958

IRVINA HOLMAN
County Home Demonstration Agent

In 1948, Johnny and Era Flynn, assisted by Delbert Glenn, once again arranged for the company Christmas party in the theater. Bill Gipson directed the carolers' chorus, and Santa Claus, played by reliable C.C. Sandy, passed out gifts to some 100 youngsters. In 1950, Leonard Lee was master of ceremonies, and because the theater had burned, the event took place at the Texon Church, where it continued to be held. Lee is pictured with Santa (Sandy) and Bill Humphrey. The date of the 1955 party was earlier than the customary Christmas Eve because so many families traveled over the holidays, and Jimmy Potter served as the jolly fellow in red that year. Company support ended after the 1956 party, and although residents gathered in 1957 for a covered dish supper and Santa's presents, another tradition had passed. (Johnny Flynn.)

Angie Fell Hasty, raised in Texon, authored the following poem long after she left, probably in the late 1970s or 1980s:

TEXON

Yes, it is a town I seek-
As a tear rolls down my cheek;
Where have the streets and houses gone?
Have I been away so long?
I walk around but do not see
A friend or neighbor to greet me;
I look but cannot find-
That old school house of mine;
Where is the church that stood so proud
When inside there was a crowd?
Where are the friends and neighbors now?
That I would like to see some how?
And as I go upon the hill
The swimming pool with dirt is filled;
And where once was the picnic ground,
Tumble weeds are all around.
I seek but cannot find,
That old hometown of mine;
Yes, it has been laid to rest,
But from its roots have grown the best—
Teachers, lawyers, an architect,
Preachers, authors, a poet yet;
For each has gone his separate way,
To become what he is today,
And as the years roll by
Each will remember with a sigh-
For their memories are drawn
To their old home town "TEXON."

Four

THE LEGACY

The Texon reunion is proof positive of a community spirit. On the first weekend in June, former residents from across Texas and the nation bring their spouses, children, grandchildren, and great-grandchildren to take in the Texon experience, to once again become a community, and to enjoy each other. The annual gathering is a sharing of memories, accompanied by laughter, appreciation, and even tears. Bertha Delz, Texon's last postmaster, told a San Angelo newspaper columnist that the reunion is an opportunity for "people to renew . . . memories." Those shared memories, along with photographs, memorabilia, films, slides, oral presentations, and tours of the townsite, make Texon come alive.

Family is a constant theme in reunion conversation—families helping families, families fishing and picnicking together, and families attending church and school functions. Here, children were able to receive guidance from their own parents and those of their friends. The BLOC's sponsorship of family-oriented activities, its kindness toward families facing hardship, and its generosity toward returning veterans were all noteworthy characteristics of this former company town.

Community and family go a long way in describing what Texon was—and its legacy.

The first Texon reunion occurred in 1964. Because they missed the "good old days," Bertha Delz and Fern Kosel, who still lived in Texon, decided it was time for a homecoming. They and former residents in Big Lake and San Angelo made the arrangements and spread the word. On Saturday and Sunday, June 13 and 14, more than 500 gathered at the newer picnic grounds to greet old friends, reminisce, and consume lots of food. Until 1976, two-day reunions were biennial and then yearly, with the venue shifting to Big Lake's Community Center. In 2010, for the first time, the reunion was held on Saturday only. Paul McCollum is pictured at left addressing the 1964 crowd. McCollum, an Odessa attorney, emceed every reunion until his death in 2004. People wait patiently for food in the image below. (Photographs by BT.)

Pictured above at the first Texon reunion are former Texon schoolteachers. They are, from left to right, Paul Carroll, Irene Teele, Norine Menielle, Lilla Beyer, Crystal Smith, Marie McCollum, Nan Day, and Alla Pool. Below are teachers and their former Texon School students. (Photographs by BT.)

Texon Oilers of the 1930s got together at the 1964 reunion. Pictured above are, from left to right, Baldy Joiner, Cotton Kerlin, Curtis Barbee, Wally Ritter, Roy Gardner, Putsy Gentry, Flop Harris, and Snipe Conley. The three attendees below are, from left to right, Theodore Wilson, Cliff Newbrough, and C.A. Jones. (Photographs by BT.)

In 1926, W.F. "Bill" Thompson, along with his mother, brother, three sisters, and grandfather, arrived in Texon to join his brother Raymond. BLOC employed him first as a PBX operator then moved him to the accounting department alongside his brother Jesse. Photography, however, became his calling, and Thompson captured on film the growth of Texon and the Big Lake Field. When he and Jesse transferred to Sinton in 1936, Texon lost its visual historian. Thompson became a photographer for Plymouth's monthly publications, the *Loose Leaf* and the *Pioneer*. When he and his brothers retired, their service to Plymouth-BLOC totaled 100 years. (Photograph by Walt Hawkins, courtesy BT.)

In 1958, the Santa Fe Railway retired the Texon depot, a No. 3 Branch Line Standard Depot. L.B. Barefoot bought the 24-by-64-foot building and moved it to Sheffield, in Pecos County, to become a feed store. Yvonne McComb of Rankin, its next owner, sold it in October 2002 to Jane McAfee, who moved it to her home in West Odessa and restored it. Today, it is the private Texon Santa Fe Depot Museum and is open to visitors by appointment. (Photograph by James A. Wilson.)

In his spare time, Marathon retiree Joe Kosel, a former Oiler and BLOC rig builder, made a scale model (one inch equal to one foot) of Santa Rita No. 1, pictured in 1984. A 400-revolutions-per-minute motor powers the pump. Kosel, far right, displayed his creation at Texon reunions in the late 1970s and 1980s. Its permanent home is the Hickman Museum in Big Lake. At this 1984 reunion, attendance totaled 250 people. (Photograph by James A. Wilson.)

Texon schoolteacher Martin W. Schwettmann wrote his master's thesis on Santa Rita No. 1 under Walter Prescott Webb, distinguished University of Texas historian. Webb suggested that the Santa Rita works be moved to the Austin campus, and BLOC's Charles Beyer agreed. In January 1940, Tom Reed's rig builders—Earl Brooks, Joe Kosel, Howard Maris, Barney May, and James Williams—dismantled the rig and pump, which were shipped by rail to Austin and stored beneath the stands of Memorial Stadium. War intervened, the timbers rotted, and it was not until November 1958 that the remaining parts were relocated to a site on Nineteenth Street (now Martin Luther King Street) and dedicated. (Photograph by James A. Wilson.)

Visit us at
arcadiapublishing.com

....

www.ingramcontent.com/pod-product-compliance
Lightning Source LLC
Chambersburg PA
CBHW050601110426

42813CB00008B/2429